W0111359

Macmillan Computer Science Series
Consulting Editor Professor F.H. Sumner, University of Manchester

S.T. Allworth and R.N. Zobel, *Introduction to Real-time Software Design, second edition*
Ian O. Angell and Gareth Griffith, *High-resolution Computer Graphics Using FORTRAN 77*
Ian O. Angell and Gareth Griffith, *High-resolution Computer Graphics Using Pascal*
M. Azmoodeh, *Abstract Data Types and Algorithms*
C. Bamford and P. Curran, *Data Structures, Files and Databases*
Philip Barker, *Author Languages for CAL*
A.N. Barrett and A.L. Mackay, *Spatial Structure and the Microcomputer*
R.E. Berry, B.A.E. Meekings and M.D. Soren, *A Book on C, second edition*
P. Beynon-Davies, *Information Systems Development*
G.M. Birtwistle, *Discrete Event Modelling on Simula*
B.G. Blundell, C.N. Daskalakis, N.A.E. Heyes and T.P. Hopkins, *An Introductory Guide to Silvar Lisco and Hilo Simulators*
B.G. Blundell and C.N. Daskalakis, *Using and Administering an Apollo Network*
T.B. Boffey, *Graph Theory in Operations Research*
Richard Bornat, *Understanding and Writing Compilers*
Linda E.M. Brackenbury, *Design of VLSI Systems – A Practical Introduction*
G.R. Brookes and A.J. Stewart, *Introduction to occam 2 on the Transputer*
J.K. Buckle, *Software Configuration Management*
W.D. Burnham and A.R. Hall, *Prolog Programming and Applications*
P.C. Capon and P.J. Jinks, *Compiler Engineering Using Pascal*
J.C. Cluley, *Interfacing to Microprocessors*
J.C. Cluley, *Introduction to Low-level Programming for Microprocessors*
Robert Cole, *Computer Communications, second edition*
Derek Coleman, *A Structured Programming Approach to Data*
Andrew J.T. Colin, *Fundamentals of Computer Science*
Andrew J.T. Colin, *Programming and Problem-solving in Algol 68*
S.M. Deen, *Fundamentals of Data Base Systems*
S.M. Deen, *Principles and Practice of Database Systems*
C. Delannoy, *Turbo Pascal Programming*
Tim Denvir, *Introduction to Discrete Mathematics for Software Engineering*
P.M. Dew and K.R. James, *Introduction to Numerical Computation in Pascal*
D. England et al., *A Sun User's Guide*
K.C.E. Gee, *Introduction to Local Area Computer Networks*
J.B. Gosling, *Design of Arithmetic Units for Digital Computers*
M.G. Hartley, M. Healey and P.G. Depledge, *Mini and Microcomputer Systems*
Roger Hutty, *Z80 Assembly Language Programming for Students*
Roland N. Ibbett and Nigel P. Topham, *Architecture of High Performance Computers, Volume I*
Roland N. Ibbett and Nigel P. Topham, *Architecture of High Performance Computers, Volume II*
Patrick Jaulent, *The 68000 – Hardware and Software*
P. Jaulent, L. Baticle and P. Pillot, *68020-30 Microprocessors and their Coprocessors*
J.M. King and J.P. Pardoe, *Program Design Using JSP – A Practical Introduction*
E.V. Krishnamurthy, *Introductory Theory of Computer Science*
V.P. Lane, *Security of Computer-Based Information Systems*
Graham Lee, *From Hardware to Software – An Introduction To Computers*

continued overleaf

A.M. Lister and R.D. Eager, *Fundamentals of Operating Systems, fourth edition*
Tom Manns and Michael Coleman, *Software Quality Assurance*
Brian Meek, *Fortran, PL/1 and the Algols*
A. Mével and T. Guéguen, *Smalltalk-80*
R.J.Mitchell, *Microcomputer Systems Using the STE Bus*
Y. Nishinuma and R. Espesser, *UNIX – First Contact*
Pim Oets, *MS-DOS and PC-DOS – A Practical Guide, second edition*
A.J. Pilavakis, *UNIX Workshop*
Christian Queinnec, *LISP*
E.J. Redfern, *Introduction to Pascal for Computational Mathematics*
Gordon Reece, *Microcomputer Modelling by Finite Differences*
W.P. Salman, O. Tisserand and B. Toulout, *FORTH*
L.E. Scales, *Introduction to Non-linear Optimization*
Peter S. Sell, *Expert Systems – A Practical Introduction*
A.G. Sutcliffe, *Human–Computer Interface Design*
Colin J. Theaker and Graham R. Brookes, *A Practical Course on Operating Systems*
M.R. Tolhurst et al., *Open Systems Interconnection*
J-M. Trio, *8086–8088 Architecture and Programming*
A.J. Tyrrell, *COBOL from Pascal*
M.J. Usher, *Information Theory for Information Technologists*
B.S. Walker, *Understanding Microprocessors*
Colin Walls, *Programming Dedicated Microprocessors*
I.R. Wilson and A.M. Addyman, *A Practical Introduction to Pascal – with BS6192, second edition*

Non-series

Roy Anderson, *Management, Information Systems and Computers*
I.O. Angell, *Advanced Graphics with the IBM Personal Computer*
J.E. Bingham and G.W.P Davies, *Planning for Data Communications*
B.V. Cordingley and D. Chamund, *Advanced BASIC Scientific Subroutines*
N. Frude, *A Guide to SPSS/PC+*
Barry Thomas, *A PostScript Cookbook*

COBOL
From
Pascal

A.J. Tyrrell

Department of Computing
Manchester Polytechnic

MACMILLAN

First published 1989

Published by
MACMILLAN EDUCATION LTD
Houndmills, Basingstoke, Hampshire RG21 2XS
and London
Companies and representatives
throughout the world

Laserset by
Ponting–Green Publishing Services, London

British Library Cataloguing in Publication Data

Tyrrell, A.J.
    Cobol from Pascal
    1. Computer systems. Programming languages : Cobol language
    I. Title
    005.13′3

ISBN 978-0-333-48303-9   ISBN 978-1-349-10594-6 (eBook)
DOI 10.1007/978-1-349-10594-6

Contents

Preface

The COBOL language needs little introduction. Created over thirty years ago for batch data processing, COBOL has withstood major changes in hardware capabilities, new applications, and new programming ideas, and still resists all efforts to pronounce its demise. The 1985 definition of the language by the American National Standards Institute has updated the language by incorporating structured programming ideas. It remains the most widely used commercial application language, with no successor in sight. Even if the fourth generation languages undermine COBOL's commercial dominance, the existing large-scale investment in COBOL software is likely to prolong the current demand for COBOL expertise for the foreseeable future.

The idea for this book derived from experience in teaching COBOL to students who have previously learned Pascal. The COBOL texts currently available have not been well suited to this task. They tend to be over-long; they sometimes attempt to provide an introduction to the program life cycle and the programming environment as well as to COBOL; they sometimes try to locate COBOL within its application domain; they often provide lengthy examples which, although realistic and useful in themselves, are difficult for readers to follow and implement in the time normally available for learning COBOL.

This book is intended to provide a different approach. Firstly, it builds on the programming language Pascal, which has in the last decade become virtually the *lingua franca* of academic computing; secondly, it aims to take COBOL learning out of the batch/Hollerith card era and to situate it in the era of microcomputer implementations of COBOL and of interactive editing, compilation and execution of computer programs.

The book is concerned with language skills and language understanding rather than programming methodology. No mention is made of testing, debugging or documentation, and no attention given to the environment in which programs must be entered, compiled and executed. It is assumed that a reader will have been introduced to these matters previously, presumably during the acquisition of Pascal skills.

Little direct attention is given to design. The author does not believe that COBOL is the best vehicle for teaching program design, and the book assumes that a reader will have been introduced to a design methodology, presumably alongside the acquisition of Pascal skills. The book aims to reinforce and build on the structured programming methods which Pascal was created to inculcate, and it uses a Pascal-oriented pseudo code to specify program design when required.

The book is not a rule-oriented manual. It tries to provide a concise, and therefore partial, introduction to the language. It makes heavy use of short examples which can be entered, compiled and executed as an aid to active learning, using VDU input–output only. The reader is encouraged to start with a simple COBOL template, which may be reused in subsequent chapters; this should help to avoid the demoralising and time-wasting compilation errors which come from misplacing sections and paragraphs in the wrong columns when programs are entered from scratch. Each chapter includes some study suggestions and practical exercises.

The book is aimed at two types of reader: firstly, the student who has been taught programming methodology using Pascal, and is following a taught COBOL course that builds on Pascal; secondly, a graduate in computer science who has learned to program to an advanced level and is required to pick up COBOL quickly. The second type of reader ought to be able to use this text without guidance, and should certainly be able to handle the early chapters very easily.

The sequencing of material is intended to follow that which would be fairly standard in a Pascal text, apart from the early treatment of procedures, and the coverage of sequential files before arrays. This means that records and files are introduced much later than is the case in most COBOL texts. The early introduction of procedural abstraction should follow naturally from the reader's experience of Pascal. In any case there seems some advantage in introducing procedures at a very early stage before the writing of in-line code becomes ingrained, and alongside the introduction to top-down design. This reflects the importance attached to producing understandable and maintainable programs, and the relative down-grading of considerations of machine efficiency.

The book is intended to be read in the order presented, but a reader may find it possible to alter the order in which topics are covered without too much difficulty.

The first part of the book consists of three very elementary chapters designed to be covered quickly, with relatively little guidance from an instructor. These chapters introduce the fundamentals of the language, including elementary data items, and the DISPLAY, ACCEPT, MOVE, COMPUTE, ADD, MULTIPLY, DIVIDE and SUBTRACT verbs.

The second part deals with control structures; each chapter builds on a student's experience using Pascal structures. Chapter 4 introduces procedures, implemented using COBOL paragraphs and the PERFORM verb. Chapters 5 and 6 show how selection and iteration may be realised in COBOL, and also introduce condition names and class conditions.

The third part consists of six chapters with emphasis on COBOL's strengths as a file and record handling language. Chapter 7 begins with coverage of multi-level records; chapter 8 covers sequential files; chapter 9 covers data editing and provides a lengthy practical exercise involving the production of a report from a sequential file; chapters 10, 11 and 12 cover tables, indexed and relative files.

The fourth part consists of two chapters organised around modular programming. These discuss concepts of modularity, data abstraction and data hiding, and introduce the facilities provided in COBOL for the separate compilation and calling of subprograms, and for the nesting of programs.

Finally, a note on COBOL 74 and COBOL 85. At the time of writing most academic installations in the UK appear to be using ANSI 74 compilers, although the situation is changing. Irrespective of the tools available in industry, the bulk of the vast amount of existing COBOL software is written to conform to the ANSI 74 standard. For the foreseeable future COBOL programmers are likely to need a knowledge of ANSI 74 COBOL as well as an appreciation of the changes introduced in the latest standard. This book attempts to cover both standards, and to point out differences between the standards as they arise. The main differences are encountered in chapters 5 and 6, in which conditional and iterative statements are covered; the material in chapter 14 applies exclusively to the 85 standard.

The author reiterates that this is not a manual; readers are urged to check installation manuals, particularly for any implementation specific coding for environment and data division file entries, and also for instructions on compiling and linking separately compiled and nested programs.

I should like to acknowledge the advice and assistance received from lecturing staff, technical staff and students in the Department of Computing at Manchester Polytechnic, and in particular thank my colleagues Pamela Quick and Zuhair Bandar, who read the text and pointed out a number of errors of style and content.

I should also like to acknowledge the advice of Paul Layzell of UMIST and of Dave Watson of Huddersfield Polytechnic, whose comments at an early stage were particularly valuable, and of my former colleague Ed Downs, who suggested the title.

Acknowledgement

Part 1

Introduction
to COBOL

1 Language Fundamentals

This chapter seeks to introduce the COBOL language sufficiently to enable a reader to compile and execute simple programs using elementary data declarations and terminal input–output only. It also introduces concepts of division, paragraph, verb, numeric and non-numeric literal.

The chapter begins with a skeleton COBOL program. Readers who intend to develop practical skills in parallel with their use of this book should enter and compile this program which may be used as a template for subsequent exercises. This will avoid unnecessary and time-wasting debugging of common errors such as mis-spelling or faulty positioning of COBOL Divisions.

1.1 A Skeleton COBOL Program

The following Pascal program would display the two strings of characters enclosed in single quotes on successive lines of a VDU screen:

```
PROGRAM FirstProg (Input,Output);

BEGIN
    Writeln('This is my first program');
    Writeln('Program successfully terminated')
END.
```

An equivalent COBOL program may be written as follows:

```
IDENTIFICATION DIVISION.
PROGRAM-ID.  FIRSTPROG.

ENVIRONMENT DIVISION.

DATA DIVISION.

PROCEDURE DIVISION.
PARA-1.
    DISPLAY  "This is my first program".
    DISPLAY  "Program successfully terminated".
    STOP RUN.
```

Example 1.1 Structure of a COBOL program

3

COBOL is above all a file-handling language, and the program in example 1.1 is therefore an unrealistic example, but it may nevertheless be entered and executed. Before doing so we should take note of the rules for formatting the source program. The language was designed for input on 80 column cards: columns 8-11 are known as area A, and columns 12-72 are known as area B, although the rightmost margin is in fact implementation dependent. In the above example the program elements that are not indented must begin in area A, but may continue into area B. The rest should be entered in area B, with particular care against straying beyond the rightmost margin.

Failure to observe the formatting rules can lead to multiple compilation errors, so it is sensible to guard against this by setting the tab keys of the text editor to 8 and 12; a further sensible precaution is to amend a program that has already been compiled rather than enter each new program from scratch.

1.2 The Four COBOL Divisions

A Pascal program consists of a program heading, followed by an optional declaration part (not present in the above example) and a statement part. A COBOL program normally consists of four divisions, the headings for which must begin in area A (cols 8-11), as in example 1.1 above.

The *Identification* Division is used to identify the program; it consists of an obligatory program name and other optional features to identify when and by whom the program was written.

The *Environment* Division is used to specify the hardware environment in which a program is compiled and executed. Many of its features are no longer used, but it is required to define the files and external media that a program needs.

The *Data* Division is used to declare the data used by a program, including all files, record structures and variables. It is similar to the variable declaration part of a Pascal program.

The *Procedure* Division is used to encode the action or algorithm that a program performs. It is roughly equivalent to the statement part of a Pascal program. In its simplest form it may consist of a single paragraph as in example 1.1, but in most cases will consist of a number of paragraphs.

1.3 Paragraphs, Statements and Verbs

A paragraph is a sequence of statements named by a label. Paragraph names are begun in area A (cols 8-11). There is no explicit marking of the end of a paragraph.

Each statement begins with a verb, which is a reserved word which indicates the action to be performed. A statement may be terminated by an optional full stop. In addition, COBOL 85 provides terminators for a number of verbs; the terminators are formed by appending '-END' to the verb name, and are used to delimit the scope of the verb. These are introduced in succeeding chapters when appropriate.

Statements should be entered in area B (cols 12-72).

1.4 Reserved Words

In all the examples in this book reserved words are set in bold type as in example 1.1 above. There are well over 200 reserved words in COBOL (see appendix 1), but it is necessary to use only a small subset of these in order to program successfully.

Most of the reserved words in example 1.1 are those used for division headers.

The other reserved words used so far are:

PROGRAM-ID - a paragraph header which should always be present, followed by the name that the programmer wishes to give to the program.
DISPLAY - a verb which allows output to the screen, or to any other device allowed by an implementor.
STOP RUN - a two word statement which terminates execution of a program and returns control to the operating system; it may be entered at any place in the Procedure Division. The absence of STOP RUN will not be detected by a compiler. It is a statement, not a program terminator, and is therefore not comparable with the 'END.' which is required to terminate a Pascal program.

1.5 User-defined Names

There are two user-defined names in example 1.1, the program name, FIRSTPROG, and a paragraph name, PARA-1. User-defined names may be formed from letters, hyphens and digits, using at least one alphabetic character. They must not begin or end with a hyphen, and should not be longer than 30 characters. There may be additional implementor's restrictions on the formation of the program name. User-defined paragraph names may be formed without any alphabetic character, although this practice reduces program readability and should not be encouraged.

This text conforms to the 74 standard and uses only uppercase letters in user-defined words and reserved words. The 85 standard allows upper and lowercase letters to be interchanged. In COBOL 85, as in Pascal, all of the following spellings are considered identical: Read READ rEAD read. In COBOL 74 only READ is allowable.

Since the language has so many reserved words the chance of error through use of a reserved word as a user-defined name is very high; the use of hyphenated names reduces the risk of this, since very few COBOL reserved words are hyphenated.

Examples of correctly formed user-defined names:

```
READ-CUSTOMER-FILE     CONTROL-PARA      STUDENT-REC
CUSTOMER-ID            PARA1             1A
2-3Z                   C1                B
```

1.6 Screen Output

In the first program, strings of characters or non-numeric literals were written on the screen using the verb DISPLAY:

```
DISPLAY  "Program successfully terminated".
```

This verb may also be used to write a sequence of digits (called a *numeric literal* in COBOL):

```
DISPLAY  12.
```

or a combination of non-numeric and numeric literals

```
DISPLAY  12   "pounds"   50   "pence".
```

Numeric literals displayed should be unsigned integers. The simplest solution to this restriction is to convert signed or non-integral numeric literals to non-numeric by enclosing them in quotes:

```
DISPLAY  " -123.67 ".
```

There is no provision for a field-width or a tab facility. If an item is required to begin in a particular column then the required spaces must be inserted in quotes :

```
DISPLAY " " 12 " pounds " 50 "pence".
```

Most systems allow cursor control by displaying a control character followed by two co-ordinates, but this is machine dependent, and the appropriate VDU manual should be consulted.

The 85 standard provides for a WITH NO ADVANCING phrase to prevent line-feed after the statement has been executed. The following sequence of statements would output: £23.

```
DISPLAY  "£" WITH NO ADVANCING.
DISPLAY 23.
```

It should be noted that the verb DISPLAY can be used to output only literals or data items (see next section). Pascal would allow us to write expressions, so that

```
Write (6+3*2)
```

would output the value 12, but in COBOL the result of the expression would have to be calculated and stored in a data item before the display statement.

1.7   Elementary Data Declarations

So far, we have simply shown how to output numeric and non-numeric literals. We may now amend our first program to show how data-items could be declared, given an initial value, and used in a similar way to constants in Pascal.

```
IDENTIFICATION DIVISION.
PROGRAM-ID.  PROG2.

ENVIRONMENT DIVISION.

DATA DIVISION.
WORKING-STORAGE SECTION.
   01  WS-MESSAGE-1              PIC X(30)
      VALUE "This is my first COBOL program".
   01  WS-MESSAGE-2              PIC X(29)
      VALUE "PROG1 successfully terminated".
   01  WS-YEAR-OF-BIRTH          PIC 9(4)
      VALUE 1945.

PROCEDURE DIVISION.
PARA-1.
   DISPLAY  WS-MESSAGE-1.
   DISPLAY  "I was  born in"  WS-YEAR-OF-BIRTH.
   DISPLAY  WS-MESSAGE-2.
   STOP RUN.
```

Example 1.2 Elementary data declarations

It should be noted that the Working-Storage Section has now been added to the previously empty Data Division. This section is used for the declaration of data other than the files and associated records used in the program.

It may also be noted that each of the data names in example 1.2 is prefaced with WS (short for Working-Storage); this is simply a matter of programming style, but it is widely adopted and is useful in distinguishing working-storage items declared elsewhere in the Data Division.

Each data declaration must consist of a level number, a data-name formed according to the rules described in section 1.5, and a PICTURE clause. For the moment we shall assume that each data name is given the level number 1, often written as 01, and beginning in area A. The PICTURE clause, introduced by the reserved word PIC, establishes the size and type of the data item. For an alphanumeric item we may use a sequence of Xs to form the picture string as follows:

```
01   WS-NAME PIC   XXXXX.
```

Each X represents a single character, so that WS-NAME may be used to store up to five characters, eg "SMITH" or "RB123" or "12345". We may alternatively describe a five-character item as follows

```
01   WS-NAME PIC X(5).
```

To declare a numeric data item we use 9s rather than Xs:

```
01 WS-AGE   PIC 99
01 WS-DAY   PIC 9(2).
```

WS-AGE and WS-DAY will store two digits, eg 07 or 70 or 15. Data items that will hold non-integral values are introduced in chapter 3.

In example 1.2 each of the data items has a VALUE clause. The initial assignment of values to a data item is optional, but in cases when a Working-Storage item requires initialisation it should be done using a VALUE clause rather than in the Procedure Divison. It should be noted that an alphanumeric value is enclosed in quotes, but a numeric value is not.

If we wish to declare data items without initialisation the VALUE clause is omitted :

```
01   YEAR-OF-BIRTH        PIC 9(4).
01   STUDENT-NAME         PIC X(20).
```

Note that the full stop denotes the end of the sentence and is now required immediately after the PICTURE clause, whereas in example 1.2 it came at the end of the VALUE clause. It is important to position full stops correctly to avoid multiple compilation errors.

1.8 Input from the Keyboard

Keyboard input is achieved using the ACCEPT verb. The sequence of statements in example 1.2 could be altered to the following :

```
DISPLAY "Enter your date of birth".
ACCEPT  YEAR-OF-BIRTH.
DISPLAY "I was born in" YEAR-OF-BIRTH.
```

ACCEPT is similar to the Read procedure in Pascal, but allows entry of a single item only. Additionally, it may be used to obtain the date, time, day or day-of-week from the computer.

1.9 Comments

COBOL was designed to be self-documenting, and a well-written program with meaningful user-defined names should not require a large number of comments.

Comments may be inserted by writing the character * in column 7. When the compiler encounters this the rest of the line is taken as a comment.

Insertion of the / character in column 7 also allows a programmer to insert a comment and in addition produces a new page on a source code listing. This can be particularly useful for large programs; some installations insist that this facility is used to list each division on a separate page.

Study Suggestions

This chapter has introduced some of the fundamental concepts of COBOL. You are advised to re-read it if necessary to ensure that you have understood and have notes on each of the following:

divisions, verbs, paragraphs, numeric literals, non-numeric literals, PICTURE clause, VALUE clause, area A, area B, user-defined names.

Practical Exercises

1. Amend example 1.2 to accept and display a user's year of birth; run the program a number of times to see how it handles differing values such as 19   19089   123C   1908X   1900.

2. Amend the program further to make it accept a number of your attributes, eg name, age, address; run the program and investigate how it handles data entered that is larger or smaller than that set up in the appropriate picture clause.

3. Find out from your manual how the ACCEPT verb may be used to get time and date from the computer. Write a program that accepts and displays each on the screen with suitable labels.

2   Assignment Statements

This chapter discusses the concept of assignment, introduces the COBOL verbs which can be used to assign values to data items, provides extensive treatment of the MOVE verb, and introduces figurative constants. Fuller coverage of the COMPUTE verb is delayed until chapter 3.

2.1   Simple Assignment in COBOL

Imperative programming languages such as Pascal allow the programmer to store a value in an area of memory allocated to a variable data item. In Pascal the := operator is used and the item to the left of the operator is assigned the result of an expression to the right of the operator. Given the following Pascal declarations:

```
VAT, UnitCost, Quantity : Integer;
CustomerName : PACKED ARRAY[1..15] OF Char;
```

the following sequence of assignments would be possible:

```
CustomerName := 'Smith
UnitCost := 16;
Quantity := 5;
VAT := UnitCost * Quantity * 15 / 100;
```

In the first three cases a constant value is assigned, but in the final case the result of an expression is assigned. The first three may be done in COBOL using the MOVE verb (see example 2.1), which is more like an assembly language operator than a high level assignment operator; the fourth assignment requires a different solution using the COMPUTE verb (example 2.2).

```
IDENTIFICATION DIVISION.
PROGRAM-ID.  ASSIGN1.

ENVIRONMENT DIVISION.

DATA DIVISION.
WORKING-STORAGE SECTION.
    01 WS-CUSTOMER-NAME     PIC X(15).
    01 WS-VAT               PIC 999.
    01 WS-UNIT-COST         PIC 99.
    01 WS-QUANTITY          PIC 999.
PROCEDURE DIVISION.
PARA-1.
    MOVE  "Smith"  TO  WS-CUSTOMER-NAME.
    MOVE 16  TO  WS-UNIT-COST.
    MOVE  5  TO  WS-QUANTITY.
    STOP RUN.
```

Example 2.1 Assignment using MOVE verb

The first statement will fill the receiving field, WS-CUSTOMER-NAME as follows,

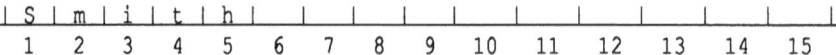

```
 | S | m | i | t | h |   |   |   |   |    |    |    |    |    |    |
   1   2   3   4   5   6   7   8   9  10   11   12   13   14   15
```

with no need therefore to pad out the source string with spaces as would be required in Pascal.

In the second and third cases involving numeric data items WS-UNIT-COST and WS-QUANTITY the result will be as follows:

```
 | 1 | 6 |                        | 0 | 0 | 5 |
   1   2                            1   2   3

WS-UNIT-COST                      WS-QUANTITY
```

Note that in last case the leading spaces are filled with zeros.

In the fourth case it would not be possible to use the verb MOVE without first evaluating the right hand of the assignment statement. The MOVE verb cannot itself evaluate an expression and then move the result. The simplest solution is to use the COMPUTE verb, which may be considered the equivalent of the assignment operator for numeric expressions:

```
IDENTIFICATION DIVISION.
PROGRAM-ID.  ASSIGN2.

ENVIRONMENT DIVISION.

DATA DIVISION.
WORKING-STORAGE SECTION.
   01 WS-CUSTOMER-NAME  PIC X(15).
   01 WS-VAT            PIC 999.
   01 WS-UNIT-COST      PIC 99.
   01 WS-QUANTITY       PIC 999.
PROCEDURE DIVISION.
PARA-1.
   MOVE 16  TO  WS-UNIT-COST.
   MOVE  5  TO  WS-QUANTITY.
    COMPUTE WS-VAT = WS-UNIT-COST
              * WS-QUANTITY * 15 / 100.
   STOP RUN.
```

Example 2.2 Assigning an arithmetic expression using COMPUTE verb

The value stored in WS-VAT as a result of the above statement would be:

0	0	1	2
1	2	3	4

We may now summarise the facilities available in COBOL for assignment:

1. The verb MOVE may be used for assignment of a constant value or a data item to one or more data items. Further coverage of this verb is given in the next section of this chapter.
2. The verb COMPUTE may be used for assignment of the result of arithmetic expressions to one or more data items. Further coverage of this verb is given in chapter 3.
3. Other arithmetic verbs (ADD DIVIDE MULTIPLY SUBTRACT) may be used for the assignment of the results of expressions in which only one operator requires evaluation. Further coverage of these verbs is given in chapter 3.

2.2   The MOVE Verb

The MOVE verb can be used to copy a constant value to one or more data locations:

```
MOVE 17 TO  WS-UNIT-COST  WS-QUANTITY.
MOVE "JOHNSON"   TO  WS-CUSTOMER-NAME.
```

A number of figurative constants, SPACE, SPACES, ZERO, ZEROS are available and may also be used in this way:

```
MOVE ZEROS TO  WS-NUMBER-1  WS-NUMBER-2.
MOVE SPACES TO  WS-CUSTOMER-NAME.
MOVE ZEROS TO WS-MONTH  WS-DAY  WS-YEAR.
```

It should be noted that the figurative constant SPACE (or SPACES) may not be moved to a numeric data item. Both SPACES and ZEROS may of course be moved to an alphanumeric (PIC X) data item.

There is also a reserved word ALL, which may be used with a MOVE, to fill a data item with a single character.

```
MOVE ALL "X" TO WS-NAME.
```

would move an uppercase X to each character position in WS-NAME, and

```
MOVE ALL "_" TO WS-LINE.
```

would move an underline character to each character position in WS-LINE. The MOVE verb may also be used to copy the value of one data-name to one or more data-names:

```
MOVE WS-NUMBER-1 TO WS-UNIT-COST  WS-QUANTITY.
```

2.3 Rules for use of MOVE

It should be noted that, whereas a Pascal compiler enforces strict type checking rules, a COBOL compiler allows a programmer more flexibility, and serious errors may be caused by careless use of the MOVE verb. A particular source of error derives from moves in which the receiving data item is smaller than the source.

The rules for moves in which the receiving field is numeric differ from those in which the receiving field is non-numeric:

i) Numeric Receiving Field

For integral values the receiving field is right justified.

If the source field is larger than the receiving field then significant digits will be lost. For example, a move from a data item containing the value 6000 to a data item declared as a PIC 9(3) item, will transfer only the three rightmost digits:

6	0	0	0
1	2	3	4

Source

0	0	0
1	2	3

Target

If the receiving field is larger than the source field then the leading positions are filled with zeros. So the move from a data item containing 20 to a PIC 9(4) field will leave the receiving field with the value 0020.

2	0
1	2

Source

0	0	2	0
1	2	3	4

Target

Moves to non-integral data items are covered in chapter 3.

ii) Non-numeric Receiving Field

The receiving item is filled from left to right. Truncation occurs if the source data item or value is larger than the receiving item. For example, an attempt to move an item 23 characters long to a PIC X(12) data item will transfer the first 12 characters only:

```
|J|A|M|E|S| |R|O|B|E|R|T|S|O|N| |J|U|S|T|I|C|E|
                    1 1 1 1 1 1 1 1 1 1 2 2 2 2
1 2 3 4 5 6 7 8 9 0 1 2 3 4 5 6 7 8 9 0 1 2 3
```

```
|J|A|M|E|S| |R|O|B|E|R|T|
                    1 1 1
1 2 3 4 5 6 7 8 9 0 1 2
```

If the receiving item is larger than the source field then the rightmost positions in the receiving item are filled with spaces, so that a move back to to a PIC X(23) data item would have the following effect:

```
|J|A|M|E|S| |R|O|B|E|R|T| | | | | | | | | | | |
                    1 1 1 1 1 1 1 1 1 1 2 2 2 2
1 2 3 4 5 6 7 8 9 0 1 2 3 4 5 6 7 8 9 0 1 2 3
```


Study Suggestions

You are advised to make notes on the use of the MOVE verb for assigning non-numeric and integral values.

Practical Exercises

1. Amend the program given in example 2.1 to make it accept values for unit-cost and quantity from the keyboard and output on the screen the total goods cost and the overall total (total goods + VAT).

2. Given the following declarations:

```
01 WS-SUBJECT        PIC X(6).
01 WS-STUDENT-ID     PIC 9(6).
01 WS-LECTURER       PIC X(2).
01 WS-EXAM           PIC 99.
01 WS-COURSE-WORK    PIC 99.
```

work out the expected result of each of the following moves in the order given below.

```
1.    MOVE "AB123" TO WS-SUBJECT.
2.    MOVE WS-SUBJECT TO WS-LECTURER.
3.    MOVE WS-LECTURER TO WS-SUBJECT.
4.    MOVE 197 TO WS-EXAM.
5.    MOVE "JRR" TO WS-LECTURER  WS-SUBJECT.
6.    MOVE 102634 TO WS-STUDENT-ID.
7.    MOVE WS-STUDENT-ID TO WS-SUBJECT.
8.    MOVE WS-STUDENT-ID TO  WS-EXAM WS-COURSE-WORK.
```

The results can be checked by writing and implementing a COBOL program which does each of the moves and displays the target item(s) on completion of each move.

3 Arithmetic Operations

This chapter provides further treatment of the COMPUTE verb, and introduces fixed-point arithmetic and signed fields. Section 2 provides an introduction to facilities available for handling overflow and also offers a first look at the use of statement terminators in COBOL 85. The final section deals with the arithmetic verbs ADD, SUBTRACT, MULTIPLY and DIVIDE; this section may be omitted on a first reading, since use of the COMPUTE verb is adequate for all arithmetic operations and is simple to pick up for those with a grounding in Pascal and other high level languages.

3.1 The COMPUTE Verb

The COMPUTE verb provides a simple way of performing all arithmetic assignments. When using the COMPUTE verb the operators and rules of precedence are virtually the same as in Pascal:

```
high (      )
         *  /              (no DIV or MOD available)
low  +  -
```

No DIV operator is available, but the / operator will produce equivalent results

```
COMPUTE  WS-RESULT = 15/4
```

will store 3 in the data item WS-RESULT. The results may be rounded up as follows

```
COMPUTE  WS-RESULT ROUNDED = 15/4.
```

Care must be taken to ensure that the data items used in the computed expression as well as target data items to the left of the = operator are declared as numeric (PIC 9) items.

17

```
        IDENTIFICATION DIVISION.
        PROGRAM-ID.  ARITH1.

        ENVIRONMENT DIVISION.

        DATA DIVISION.
        WORKING-STORAGE SECTION.
           01 WS-UNIT-COST              PIC  99.
           01  WS-QUANTITY              PIC  999.
           01  WS-TOTAL-COST            PIC  9(5).
           01  WS-VAT-RATE              PIC  99.

        PROCEDURE DIVISION.
        PARA-1.
            ACCEPT  WS-UNIT-COST.
            ACCEPT  WS-QUANTITY.
            ACCEPT  WS-VAT-RATE.
            COMPUTE WS-TOTAL-COST ROUNDED =
                    WS-UNIT-COST * WS-QUANTITY  +
                    WS-UNIT-COST * WS-QUANTITY
                                 * WS-VAT-RATE / 100.
            DISPLAY  WS-TOTAL-COST.
            STOP RUN.
```

Example 3.1 Use of COMPUTE

The program in example 3.1 reads three values from the keyboard for unit cost, quantity, and VAT rate, calculates total cost by multiplying cost by quantity and adding VAT, and outputs the final cost.

3.2 Range Errors

In Pascal the attempt to assign a value outside the range of integers represented will lead to a fatal run-time overflow error. In COBOL the error will not be reported, but the result will be seriously inaccurate. For example, given the following declaration:

```
   01  WS-RESULT  PIC 999.
```

The calculation

```
   COMPUTE WS-RESULT = 25 * 500
```

will store the following:

```
| 5 | 0 | 0 |
```

in WS-RESULT because the data item can hold only three digits, and the most significant digits are lost.

This problem can be minimised by trying to ensure that the picture size of items is large enough to hold all likely values; in example 3.2 the first COMPUTE statement will never overflow because WS-TOTAL is large enough to hold the product of 999 and 99999. The second statement will overflow however if WS-TOTAL contains 99999999 before the statement is executed. After execution it will contain 00000000.

```
IDENTIFICATION DIVISION.
PROGRAM-ID.  OVFLOW.

ENVIRONMENT DIVISION.

DATA DIVISION.
WORKING-STORAGE SECTION.
    01 WS-TOTAL               PIC  9(8).
    01 WS-NUMBER-1            PIC  999.
    01 WS-NUMBER-2            PIC  9(5).
PROCEDURE DIVISION.
PARA-1.
    ........
    COMPUTE WS-TOTAL =  WS-NUMBER-1 * WS-NUMBER-2.
    ......
    COMPUTE WS-TOTAL =  WS-TOTAL + 1.
    .......
```

Example 3.2 Problems of arithmetic overflow

For such situations there is an error detection facility available. Building in error reporting saves time during program implementation and testing, and provides greater confidence about the quality of software delivered. The above calculation could be made secure using a program like example 3.3.

If overflow occurred, the effect of the ON SIZE ERROR clause in example 3.3 would be to report the state of each data item involved; if no overflow occurred, the line of code following the NO-SIZE ERROR would be executed.

Example 3.3 provides our first introduction to the use of statement terminators in COBOL 85. END-COMPUTE and NOT SIZE ERROR are optional in COBOL 85, and not available in previous standards. Their use helps to simplify structure and should help eliminate errors. In COBOL 74 the same effect could be achieved as shown in example 3.4.

```
IDENTIFICATION DIVISION.
PROGRAM-ID.  OVFLOW.
ENVIRONMENT DIVISION.
DATA DIVISION.
WORKING-STORAGE SECTION.
   01 WS-TOTAL                  PIC   9(8).
   01 WS-NUMBER-1               PIC   999.
   01 WS-NUMBER-2               PIC   9(5).
PROCEDURE DIVISION.
PARA-1.

   ...............
   COMPUTE WS-TOTAL =  WS-TOTAL + 1
      ON SIZE ERROR
         DISPLAY "Arithmetic overflow :WS-TOTAL"
         DISPLAY "WS-TOTAL =>"  WS-TOTAL
         DISPLAY "WS-NUMBER-1 =>"  WS-NUMBER-1
         DISPLAY "WS-NUMBER-2 =>"  WS-NUMBER-2
      NOT SIZE ERROR
         DISPLAY "Result => "  WS-TOTAL.
   END-COMPUTE
   ..................
```

Example 3.3 Handling arithmetic overflow (COBOL 85 only)

```
IDENTIFICATION DIVISION.
PROGRAM-ID.  OVFlow.
ENVIRONMENT DIVISION.
DATA DIVISION.
WORKING-STORAGE SECTION.
   01 WS-TOTAL                  PIC   9(8).
   01 WS-NUMBER-1               PIC   999.
   01 WS-NUMBER-2               PIC   9(5).

      ............
PROCEDURE DIVISION.
PARA-1.

   ...............
   COMPUTE WS-TOTAL =  WS-TOTAL + 1
      ON SIZE ERROR
         DISPLAY "Arithmetic overflow:WS-TOTAL"
         DISPLAY "WS-TOTAL =>"  WS-TOTAL
         DISPLAY "WS-NUMBER1 =>"  WS-NUMBER1
         DISPLAY "WS-NUMBER-2 =>"  WS-NUMBER-2
         STOP RUN.
   DISPLAY "Result => "  WS-TOTAL.
```

Example 3.4 Handling Arithmetic Overflow, COBOL 74

In example 3.4 the line of code that reports the correct result is not part of the COMPUTE statement; the COMPUTE and the SIZE ERROR statements end with the full stop after STOP RUN. Were the STOP RUN to be omitted, then the full stop would need to be at the end of the preceding line, and the final line would always be executed; to avoid this, the programmer would need to do the following:

i) replace the STOP RUN with a MOVE statement which sets an error flag.
ii) make the next statement a conditional one, executed only when the error flag had not been set;
iii) ensure that the error flag is reinitialised after an error has been detected and processed.

3.3 Fixed-point Arithmetic

So far, all arithmetic declarations have been confined to integral values. COBOL provides for fixed-point arithmetic, and items which require a decimal point should be declared using a V (virtual point) in the picture clause.

The data declarations in example 3.1 could be modified to allow unit-cost and overall-cost to store pounds and pence as shown in example 3.5

```
DATA DIVISION.
WORKING-STORAGE SECTION.
    01 WS-UNIT-COST          PIC    99V99.
    01 WS-QUANTITY           PIC    999.
    01 WS-TOTAL-COST         PIC    9(5)V99.
```

Example 3.5 Use of virtual point in data declarations

The declaration in example 3.5 allows values in the range 00.00 to 99.99 to be stored in WS-UNIT-COST, and values in the range 00000.00 to 99999.99 to be stored in WS-TOTAL-COST. Within the range allowed, complete accuracy is provided.

All calculations and moves involving items containing a virtual point will be aligned on the point.

MOVE 1000.012 **TO** WS-TOTAL-COST

would give the following:

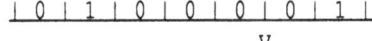
V

```
COMPUTE WS-TOTAL-COST = 0.5 * 1.5
```

would give

| 0 | 0 | 0 | 0 | 0 | 7 | 5 |
                         V

and

```
COMPUTE WS-TOTAL-COST = WS-TOTAL-COST + 210001.5
```

would give

| 1 | 0 | 0 | 0 | 2 | 2 | 5 |
                         V

with the loss of the most significant digit.

It should be noted that the point is not stored in the data item. If a user is entering a number via the keyboard into an item with a virtual point, the point itself should not be entered. To enter a unit-cost of 7.12 into WS-UNIT-COST the user would normally be required to enter 0712. Entry of 7.12 would store an incorrect value.

For programs involving keyboard input, data validation is required to guard against errors of this kind, and it would be sensible to enter a number into an alphanumeric data item and check its validity before moving it to WS-UNIT-COST.

3.4   Signed Arithmetic

If we wish an item to be capable of storing negative values an S must be included in the picture string as either the first or last character:

```
01   WS-CUSTOMER-BALANCE      PIC S999V.99.
01   WS-CURRENT-TOTAL         PIC 999V.99S.
```

The above declarations will store values in the range -999.99 to +999.99. It should be noted that the sign is not stored in a separate character, and its mode of representation is implementation defined. For portable programs the use of a SIGN clause is recommended (see your manual). If we wish to print or display signed values then we would normally move them first to a numeric edited item with appropriate sign characters (see chapter 9).

3.5   Arithmetic Verbs

Four arithmetic verbs ADD, SUBTRACT, MULTIPLY and DIVIDE, are available. The presence of these verbs is an indication of the age of COBOL and of its similarity in some respects to the assembly language that it was designed to replace.

As has previously been indicated, the verb COMPUTE is adequate for all possible computation and should be easy to use by those with experience of Pascal and other high-level languages. It also has the advantage over the other verbs that expressions which include more than one operation may be evaluated in a single sentence. For example, arithmetic assignments such as

```
COMPUTE  COMMISSION =  COMMISSION + PRICE * RATE / 100
```

would otherwise require a separate statement for each operator

```
MULTIPLY  PRICE  BY  RATE GIVING TEMP-VALUE.
DIVIDE 100 INTO TEMP-VALUE.
ADD TEMP-VALUE TO COMMISSION.
```

The COBOL programmer is likely to need to use the arithmetic verbs or at least be able to understand how they are used. The programmer should also be warned that the evaluation of arithmetic expressions is implementation dependent, so that use of the four arithmetic verbs is safer for portable programs. This section provides a short introduction to their use which may be omitted on a first reading.

Using the following data declarations,

```
01 WS-UNIT-COST          PIC   99V99.
01 WS-QUANTITY           PIC   999.
01 WS-TOTAL-COST         PIC   9(5)V99.
01 WS-VAT-COST           PIC   99V99.
01 WS-REMAINDER          PIC   999.
```

each verb may be used as follows:

```
ADD  WS-VAT-COST TO  WS-TOTAL-COST.
ADD 6 TO  WS-QUANTITY.
ADD  WS-UNIT-COST  WS-VAT-COST  TO WS-TOTAL-COST.
MULTIPLY WS-UNIT-COST BY WS-QUANTITY.
MULTIPLY 16 BY WS-UNIT-COST.
DIVIDE WS-QUANTITY INTO WS-TOTAL-COST.
```

```
DIVIDE 6 INTO WS-TOTAL-COST.
SUBTRACT WS-VAT-COST FROM WS-TOTAL-COST.
SUBTRACT WS-UNIT-COST WS-VAT-COST FROM
       WS-TOTAL-COST.
SUBTRACT 6 FROM WS-QUANTITY.
```

In each of the above cases the result of the operation would be stored in the last data name which follows reserved words TO, BY, INTO or FROM.

As would be expected, all data items must be numeric, and all literals must be numeric literals.

It is also possible to store the result of a calculation in a specified data name using the reserved word GIVING:

```
ADD WS-UNIT-COST TO WS-VAT-COST GIVING WS-TOTAL-COST.
```

This is advantageous in cases in which a programmer wishes to leave each of the operands unaffected by the operation, or cases in which both operands are literals:

```
ADD 16.5 TO 20.6 GIVING WS-TOTAL.
```

The GIVING option may be used with each of the other verbs. An added advantage of this option is that the result may be placed in an elementary numeric edited item (see chapter 9).

An additional facility is available with the DIVIDE verb to store a remainder in a specified data name:

```
DIVIDE 25 BY 6 GIVING WS-QUANTITY REMAINDER WS-REMAINDER.
```

Using COMPUTE would require two statements,

```
COMPUTE WS-QUANTITY =   25/6.
COMPUTE WS-REMAINDER = 25 - WS-QUANTITY * 6.
```

but would give no problems to most programmers.

ROUNDED and ON SIZE ERROR may also be used with the arithmetic verbs:

```
ADD  WS-UNIT-COST  WS-VAT-COST  TO WS-TOTAL-COST ROUNDED.
ADD  WS-UNIT-COST  WS-VAT-COST  TO WS-TOTAL-COST
        ON SIZE ERROR
           DISPLAY "Error: WS-TOTAL-COST overflow"
        NOT SIZE ERROR
           DISPLAY "Result => " WS-TOTAL-COST
END-ADD
```

Readers should note that the last example uses END-ADD and NOT SIZE ERROR which are available in COBOL 85 only.

Study Suggestions

This chapter has dealt with the COMPUTE, ADD, SUBTRACT, DIVIDE and MULTIPLY verbs, and has introduced the ROUNDED and ON SIZE ERROR facilities, the declaration and manipulation of numeric items containing decimal points, and signed fields. It has also given the first example of the use of statement terminators provided by COBOL 85.

You are advised to make notes initially on the use of COMPUTE and the ROUNDED and ON SIZE ERROR options. You should also make notes on the use of items containing decimal points (including the effects of the MOVE verb).

Practical Exercises

1. A program accepts values from the keyboard for each of the following: Balance-Owing, Goods-Debited, Amount-Paid. Each field is non-integral. Balance-Owing is a signed field, and is calculated by subtracting Amount-Paid from Goods-Debited. Write and test a COBOL program which will accept all three values and output the value contained in Balance-Owing.
2. Build in code that will detect when Balance-Owing overflows; test it by initialising Balance-Owing with a value near to its maximum range.
3. A trawler catch of fish is divided as follows: skipper 10%; mate and engineer 5% each; three deck hands, 2.5% each. Code a program which accepts a value for the fish sold and prints out the share of each crew member, and the balance belonging to the owners. Results should be rounded. Each value should be non-integral. A trawler catch is in the range £10,000–£25,000.

Part 2

Program
Structures

4 Procedural Abstraction

This chapter shows how the rough equivalent of a Pascal procedure can be implemented by using the PERFORM verb and partitioning solution elements into paragraphs. The chapter also introduces the use of sections, which could well be omitted on a first reading.

4.1 Introduction to use of Procedures

All modern software design methods propose some means of breaking down problems into manageable units, and it is generally easier to code programs in a similar way if the target language allows.

Procedural abstraction facilitates a top-down or hierarchical approach to algorithm design and implementation; it allows a programmer to break a problem down into manageable steps, to postpone design decisions, to hide detail, and to implement and test one procedure at a time. COBOL provides useful facilities for procedural abstraction which allow a hierarchical design to be mapped directly on to a COBOL Procedure Division.

This process can be illustrated by sketching first a Pascal example with empty procedures and then later showing how a similar COBOL solution could be produced.

The sequence of three statements in the main program in example 4.1 provides an abstract solution to the problem; detail as to how the individual statements are implemented is hidden from the top level of the program. It would be possible to encode the complete solution in the main program without any procedures and, on arguments of efficiency alone, that would be the best solution; but it is easier to implement and maintain a program with a well-defined, hierarchical structure, and this is particularly the case with larger, more realistic programs.

4.2 Paragraphs and the PERFORM Verb

An approximate COBOL equivalent to a procedure or subroutine is the paragraph which may be called by use of the PERFORM verb. There are a

```
PROGRAM   ProduceInvoice (Input,Output);

(*Data for the program not yet declared*)
(*each procedure is a template only *)

    PROCEDURE  InputItems;
    (*This procedure accepts up to 5 item codes and the
    unit-costs and quantity for each item from the keyboard*)
    BEGIN

    END;   (*InputItems*)

    PROCEDURE  CalculateCost;
    (*This procedure calculates the cost of each item,adding
      VAT and the invoice total*)
    BEGIN
    END;   (*CalculateCost*)



    PROCEDURE  PrintInvoice;
    (*This procedure prints an invoice*)
    BEGIN

    END;   (*PrintInvoice*)

BEGIN
    InputItems;
    CalculateCost;
    PrintInvoice
END. (*ProduceInvoice*)
```

Example 4.1 Use of procedures in Pascal

number of variations of the way that the PERFORM verb can be used, but at its simplest it produces a single procedure call. When a called paragraph has been executed control returns to the statement after the PERFORM statement, in precisely the same way as a Pascal procedure call. Like a procedure, a paragraph has a single exit and single entry point. No return statement is required in the called paragraph. The end of a paragraph is indicated either by the presence of the next paragraph declaration in area A (cols 8-11) or by the end of the source text.

Example 4.2 shows how a paragraph may call one paragraph which itself calls another.

```
CONTROL-PARA.
    . . . . . . . . . . . .
    PERFORM PARA-1B.
    DISPLAY " Para 1B has been executed".
    STOP RUN.
PARA-1A.
    . . . . . . . . . . . .
PARA-1B.
    . . . . . . . . . . . . .
    PERFORM PARA-1C.
    DISPLAY "This is the last sentence of Para 1B".
PARA-1C.
    . . . . . . . . . . . .
    DISPLAY "This is the last sentence of Para 1C".
PARA-1D
    . . . . . . . . . . . .
```

Example 4.2 Use of PERFORM verb

The program fragment of example 4.2 would terminate after producing the following output:

This is the last sentence of Para 1C
This is the last sentence of Para 1B
Para 1B has been executed

4.3   Implementation of a Hierarchical Program in COBOL

In example 4.1 the concepts of procedural abstraction and hierarchical structure were illustrated with a simple example implemented in Pascal. Example 4.3 shows how an equivalent COBOL Procedure Division could be implemented.

It should be noted that whereas in Pascal the main program is positioned below the procedure declarations, in COBOL the main or control paragraph is the first paragraph in the Procedure Division.

It is important that the last statement in the main paragraph is STOP RUN. It is a common error to omit this, and this omission cannot be detected by a compiler. If omitted each paragraph below the main paragraph would be executed a second time.

```
PROCEDURE DIVISION.
MAIN-PARA.
      PERFORM INPUT-ITEMS.
      PERFORM CALCULATE-COSTS.
      PERFORM PRINT-INVOICE.
      STOP RUN.

*     Each lower level at present consists solely of a stub

INPUT-ITEM.
*     This paragraph accepts from the keyboard up to 5 item codes
*     and for each item the unit-cost and quantity
      DISPLAY "Input-Item paragraph called"

CALCULATE-COSTS.
*     This paragraph calculates the cost of each item, adding VAT
*     and the invoice total
      DISPLAY "Calculate-Costs paragraph called"

PRINT-INVOICE.
*     This paragraph prints an invoice
      DISPLAY "Print-Invoice paragraph called"
```

Example 4.3 Hierarchical implementation using PERFORM

Among the common errors made by beginners are the following:

1. Inconsistent spelling of a paragraph name resulting in a compilation error at the line on which the PERFORM occurs.
2. Wrong column positioning of a paragraph declaration – it must begin in area A(cols 8-11).
3. Omission of the full stop at the end of the paragraph name declaration.

Example 4.3 consists of a simple sequence, with each lower-level paragraph called only from the main paragraph. It is sensible practice to produce hierarchical structures, with calls going downwards only, but the compiler will not enforce this. In Pascal the order of declaration determines which procedure may call another procedure, in COBOL no such rule exists.

It is difficult in a large program to locate paragraphs. Many installations use a numeric sequence so that a paragraph can easily be found. It is sensible to combine this with a systematic method of ordering paragraphs.

Alternative ways of doing this can be illustrated using the hierarchy shown below.

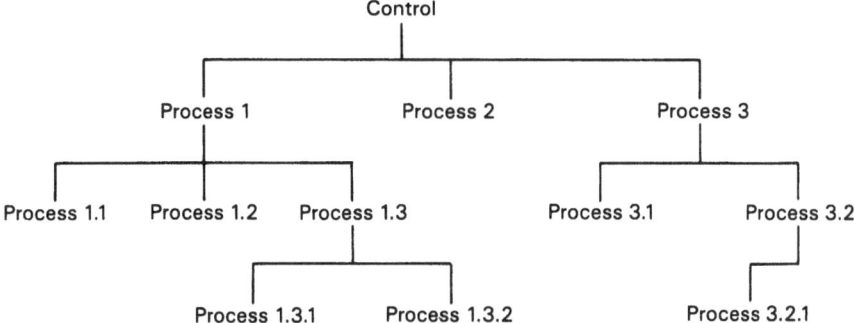

One method is to arrange the paragraphs in horizontal tiers; an alternative is to arrange them in tree order (left–right traversal), which is sometimes referred to as vertical arrangement.

```
Horizontal                    Vertical
Control                       Control

P1                            P1
P2                            P1.1
P3                            P1.2
                              P1.3
P1.1                          P1.3.1
P1.2                          P1.3.2
P1.3
                              P2
P3.1
P3.2                          P3
                              P3.1
P1.3.1                        P3.2
P1.3.2                        P3.2.1

P3.2.1
```

4.4   The Use of Sections

As an alternative to using paragraphs, the Procedure Division may be divided into sections. If sections are used then no isolated paragraphs may be declared ouside sections, and each section must contain at least one paragraph. Individual paragraphs within sections should not be called from outside the section.

The section can be used as a means of grouping under one name a number of paragraphs that are executed sequentially or alternatively as a way of partitioning a large system. In the latter case a section may well have a hierarchical structure, implemented using its own control paragraph as in example 4.4. The use of sections in this case may be preferred to the subprogram facility (see chapter 13) for reasons of efficiency, or because the modules share data.

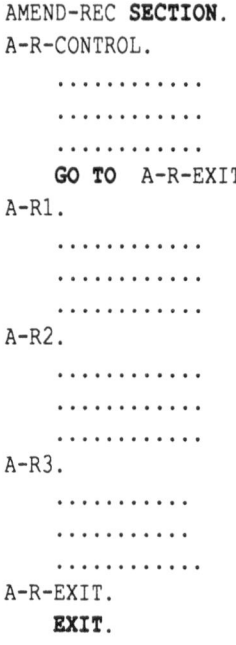

```
AMEND-REC SECTION.
A-R-CONTROL.
       . . . . . . . . . . . .
       . . . . . . . . . . . .
       . . . . . . . . . . . .
       GO TO  A-R-EXIT.
A-R1.
       . . . . . . . . . . . .
       . . . . . . . . . . . .
       . . . . . . . . . . . .
A-R2.
       . . . . . . . . . . . .
       . . . . . . . . . . . .
       . . . . . . . . . . . .
A-R3.
       . . . . . . . . . . .
       . . . . . . . . . .
       . . . . . . . . . . . .
A-R-EXIT.
       EXIT.
```

Example 4.4 Section organised hierarchically

It should be noted that a call would be made to the section, not the control paragraph

PERFORM AMEND-REC

and at that point control would be passed to the first paragraph in the called section. The control paragraph would then determine the sequence of calls within the section, and at the end would branch to the dummy final paragraph. The use of the GO TO is required for the same reason that STOP RUN is used in the control paragraph in example 4.1, to prevent re-execution of each subsequent paragraph. This is an acceptable use of the GO TO and is consistent with the structured programming requirement that each module has a single-exit single-entry. The EXIT statement is for documentation only.

4.5 Parameters and Local Data

Most modern programming languages provide some facilities for parameterised calls to subroutines and for the creation of local data as a protection against inadvertent alterations to global data. In COBOL data is global, and no parameterised calls are possible, although parameterised calls may be made to separately compiled programs (see chapter 13). COBOL 85 allows calls to nested programs which may use local and global data (see chapter 14).

Study Suggestions

The emphasis of study at this point should be on understanding how procedure equivalents can be implemented in COBOL, so that a reader can convert a top-down design into a hierarchical program.

Make a list of the differences between a Pascal procedure and a COBOL paragraph.

It would be possible to jump or GO TO a paragraph rather than PERFORM it. Why is the PERFORM considered preferable?

Compare the Pascal main program and the control paragraph in COBOL and note down the consequences of omission of the STOP RUN.

Practical Exercise

Enter, compile and execute the Procedure Division template shown in example 4.3. This program may later be completed when repetition (chapter 6) and tables (chapter 10) have been covered.

5 Control Structures 1: Selection

This chapter provides an introduction to structured programming concepts and shows how conditions and selection are implemented in COBOL 85 and COBOL 74. It also introduces class conditions and user-defined condition names.

5.1 Structured Programming

Any computable problem may be solved using a combination of the following structures:

- sequence
- selection
- iteration

Modern programming languages provide a relatively standardised and restricted set of control abstraction facilities that allow a programmer to realise selection and iteration in a clear, safe and well-defined way, and that hide the primitive statements required to control a program's flow of execution.

Pascal was developed to teach structured programming principles, and is rich in the facilities available for control abstraction. For a sequence Pascal uses the compound statement formed by enclosing simple statements within a Begin End:

```
BEGIN
      statement-1;
      .....
      statement-n
END;
```

For selection Pascal has the If statement:

```
IF condition
THEN
      statement;
```

the If Else, and the Case statement (shown in simplified form):

```
CASE selector OF
   label : statement;
   ......
   label : statement-n
END;
```

For iteration it has three structured statements, the Repeat

```
REPEAT
      statement
UNTIL condition;
```

the While statement:

```
WHILE condition DO
      statement;
```

and the For statement:

```
FOR control-variable := initial-value TO final-value DO
      statement;
```

It should be noted that there are explicit statement terminators for the Repeat and the Case but not for the If, the While or the For statements. This can lead to error; for example, if a user codes a selection as follows:

```
IF condition
THEN
   statement-1;
   statement-2;
```

statement-2 will always be executed, irrespective of the programmer's intention as indicated by the indentation. To include statement-2 within the If, a compound statement must be created, nested within the If:

```
IF condition
THEN
   BEGIN
      statement-1;
      statement-2
   END;
```

COBOL has fewer structuring facilities than Pascal, and COBOL 74 lacks any in-line repeat statements and any form of scope delimiter other than the full stop (see section 5.6 below). COBOL 85 has remedied both these deficiencies and now possesses an adequate collection of structuring facilities (see section 5.3 below).

5.2   Conditions

All alterations to the flow of execution require the evaluation of conditions which yield either a true or a false value. We may form conditions using a slightly different set of relational operators to those available in Pascal.

Relational operators COBOL 85

```
<              >=
>              <=
=              NOT =        (Equivalent to <>)
```

It should be noted that there are differences between the 85 and 74 standards: the 74 standard does not include the >= or <=, so that users of COBOL 74 must code them as

```
NOT <
NOT >.
```

Readers should also note that COBOL allows the use of English equivalents of the operators:

```
EQUAL
LESS
GREATER
GREATER OR EQUAL
LESS OR EQUAL
```

The last two are not available in the COBOL 74.

Optional 'noise words' THAN and TO are also available to make the relations more meaningful in English, so that for example

```
WS-QUANTITY > 100
```

could be coded as

```
WS-QUANTITY GREATER THAN 100
```

as well as

```
WS-QUANTITY GREATER 100
```

and

```
WS-QUANTITY = 0
```

could be coded as

```
WS-QUANTITY EQUAL TO 0.
```

Logical operators are the same as Pascal,

```
NOT
AND
OR
```

Logical operator precedence is in the order given; parentheses may be used, in which case conditions in parentheses are evaluated first. Relational operators are evaluated *before* logical operators, so that whereas in Pascal we would need to use parentheses for the following condition:

```
(NUMBER > 7)    AND   (NUMBER < 100)   OR   (NUMBER = 2000)
```

in COBOL we may omit the parentheses and write

```
NUMBER >  7    AND    NUMBER < 100   OR   NUMBER = 2000
```

There is also an abbreviated form in COBOL which allows

```
NUMBER > 7 AND < 100   OR   = 2000
```

It may however be safer to use the full form which Pascal enforces.

5.3   Selection in COBOL 85

COBOL provides an IF statement similar to that available in Pascal. It includes an optional ELSE and may be nested. There is also an optional scope delimiter, END-IF, which is useful to terminate a sequence of statements which in PASCAL would be enclosed within a Begin End.

```
IF   Pence < 1
THEN
   BEGIN

      Writeln('Error:invalid value for pence entered');
      Write('Re-enter pence>');
      Read(Pence)
   END;
   . . . . . . . . . . . .


IF   PENCE <  1
THEN
   DISPLAY "Error: invalid value for pence entered"
   DISPLAY "Re-enter pence >" WITH NO ADVANCING
   ACCEPT PENCE
END-IF.
   . . . . . . . . . . . . . . .
```

Example 5.1 Compound statement in Pascal and COBOL 85

The indentation of text is not required by the rules of the language but helps to clarify the intentions of the programmer and is recommended as an aid to readability.

The scope delimiter is particularly useful when IF statements are nested, as in example 5.2.

Without the second END-IF in example 5.2, it would be impossible to separate the statement executed after the first ELSE from the sequence of statements which follow. This problem causes difficulties in COBOL 74 and would have to be solved by moving part of the code out-of-line and using the PERFORM verb.

5.4   Multiway Selection in COBOL 85

Pascal includes a Case statement which may be used for multiway selection. For example, a simple menu driven system for a library might offer the following choices

```
        Menu

1.      Create new user
2.      Return book
3.      Renew book
4.      Loan book
5.      List user account
6.      Quit
```

The Case statement is the most appropriate abstraction for controlling the flow after an appropriate user selection has been made. When combined with procedural abstraction it provides a solution that is understandable, easily modifiable and secure, provided that unexpected values are trapped before entry.

```
CASE UserSelection OF
    "1" :  NewUser;
    "2" :  BookReturn;
    "3" :  BookRenew;
    "4" :  BookLoan;
    "5" :  ListBooksOut;
    "6" :  CloseSystem
END;
```

```
IDENTIFICATION DIVISION.
PROGRAM-ID.  IFSTMT.

ENVIRONMENT DIVISION.

DATA DIVISION.
WORKING-STORAGE SECTION.
    01 WS-QUANTITY              PIC X(4).
    01 WS-ITEM-PRICE           PIC X(4).
    01 WS-NUMERIC-QUANTITY      PIC 9(4).
    01 WS-NUMERIC-PRICE         PIC 9(4).
    01 WS-VAT-TOTAL             PIC 9(3).
    01 WS-TOTAL                 PIC 9(8).
    01 WS-CARRIAGE              PIC 9.
    01 WS-VAT-RATE              PIC 99
            VALUE 15.

PROCEDURE DIVISION.
PARA-1.
    ACCEPT WS-QUANTITY.
    ACCEPT WS-ITEM-PRICE.
    IF WS-ITEM-PRICE NUMERIC AND WS-QUANTITY NUMERIC
    THEN
        MOVE WS-QUANTITY TO WS-NUMERIC-QUANTITY
        MOVE WS-ITEM-PRICE TO WS-NUMERIC-PRICE
        COMPUTE WS-TOTAL = WS-NUMERIC-PRICE *
                               WS-NUMERIC-QUANTITY
        IF WS-TOTAL < 50
        THEN MOVE 5 TO WS-CARRIAGE
        ELSE MOVE 0 TO WS-CARRIAGE
        END-IF
        DISPLAY "Goods Total :" WS-TOTAL
        COMPUTE WS-VAT-TOTAL = WS-TOTAL *
            VAT-RATE /100
        DISPLAY "V.A.T.  :"  WS-VAT-TOTAL
        DISPLAY "CARRIAGE :" CARRIAGE
        ADD  CARRIAGE  WS-VAT-TOTAL TO WS-TOTAL
        DISPLAY "Total :"  WS-TOTAL
    ELSE DISPLAY "INVALID DATA ENTERED"
    END-IF.
    STOP RUN
```

Example 5.2 Nested IFs in COBOL 85

Some Pascal implementations also include an Otherwise statement which would allow an invalid user selection to be trapped within the Case statement. Without such a statement the above program would crash if the value held in user selection did not match any of the values listed.

The above system may readily be coded in COBOL 85 using an EVALUATE statement as shown in example 5.3. COBOL provides an optional WHEN OTHER phrase which may be used to specify the action to be taken if unanticipated conditions arise. Even if the WHEN OTHER is omitted the EVALUATE will not crash if it fails to find a match among any of the values specified.

```
IDENTIFICATION DIVISION.
PROGRAM-ID.  MSELECT1.

ENVIRONMENT DIVISION.

DATA DIVISION.
WORKING-STORAGE SECTION.
   01  USER-SELECTION            PIC X.
PROCEDURE DIVISION.
PARA-1.
     ACCEPT USER-SELECTION.
     EVALUATE USER-SELECTION
         WHEN "1" PERFORM  NEW-USER
         WHEN "2" PERFORM  BOOK-RETURN
         WHEN "3" PERFORM  BOOK-RENEW
         WHEN "4" PERFORM  BOOK-LOAN
         WHEN "5" PERFORM  LIST-BOOKS-OUT
         WHEN "6" PERFORM  CLOSE-SYSTEM
         WHEN OTHER DISPLAY "Invalid Selection"
     END-EVALUATE
     STOP RUN.
 NEW-USER.
 * This and succeeding paragraphs are templates
 BOOK-RETURN.
 BOOK-RENEW.
 BOOK-LOAN.
 LIST-BOOKS-OUT.
 CLOSE-SYSTEM.
```

Example 5.3 EVALUATE statement in COBOL 85

Example 5.3 uses the EVALUATE in a way which comes readily to a Pascal programmer. The EVALUATE statement is, however, more complicated than the Pascal equivalent as example 5.4 indicates.

```
IDENTIFICATION DIVISION.
PROGRAM-ID. MSELECT2.

ENVIRONMENT DIVISION.

DATA DIVISION.
WORKING-STORAGE SECTION.
    01  WS-PRICE              PIC 9999.
    01  WS-QUANTITY           PIC 9999.
    01  WS-MIN-QUANTITY       PIC 9
            VALUE 5.

PROCEDURE DIVISION.
PARA-1.
    ACCEPT WS-PRICE.
    ACCEPT WS-QUANTITY.
    EVALUATE  WS-PRICE  ALSO  WS-QUANTITY
        WHEN ANY ALSO 0 THROUGH WS-MIN-QUANTITY  - 1
                PERFORM  PARA-2
        WHEN 0  ALSO  ANY PERFORM  PARA-3
        WHEN  1 THROUGH 10  ALSO  WS-MIN-QUANTITY
                PERFORM  PARA-4
        WHEN NOT 100 THROUGH 200 ALSO ANY PERFORM PARA-5

        WHEN OTHER PERFORM PARA-6
    END-EVALUATE.
    STOP RUN.
PARA-2.
    DISPLAY "Quantity is below the minimum".
PARA-3.
    DISPLAY "Price = 0 ".
PARA-4.
    DISPLAY "Price in range 1 to 10".
    DISPLAY " Quantity = 5 ".
PARA-5.
    DISPLAY "Price is not in range 100-200".
PARA-6.
*  The reader should work out the conditions in which this
*  would be called
```

Example 5.4 EVALUATE using 2 selection subjects

The following points should be noted in relation to example 5.4:

- more than one data item may be evaluated; in this case there are two, WS-PRICE and WS-QUANTITY; these are known as selection subjects;
- ANY and 0 THROUGH WS-MIN-QUANTITY - 1 are known as selection objects;
- selection objects may be:
  the reserved words, TRUE, FALSE
  conditions
  ANY
  data names
  literals
  arithmetic expressions;
  these may be combined using the reserved word THROUGH, as in 0 THROUGH WS-MIN-QUANTITY - 1 in example 5.4;
- if ANY is used as an object it means that the value of the corresponding selection subject will not be considered; in example 5.4, PARA-2 would be performed if WS-QUANTITY was in the range 0 to 4, irrespective of the value of WS-PRICE;
- in each WHEN phrase there must be the same number of selection objects as there are selection subjects;
- each selection object must be compatible with the selection subject; in example 5.4 therefore we are unable to show selection objects such as TRUE, FALSE or WS-PRICE > 0, since these are not compatible with the two selection subjects chosen;
- it should be noted that when more than one selection subject is chosen both the selection objects and selection subjects are joined by the reserved word ALSO.

The Pascal Case has the advantage of simplicity, and the user is advised to bear in mind the importance of readability before using the full range of facilities that the EVALUATE has to offer. In particular it seems advisable to limit the number of selection subjects and objects used in an EVALUATE statement.

5.5 Class Conditions and Sign Conditions

COBOL provides four class conditions: NUMERIC, ALPHABETIC, ALPHABETIC-UPPER and ALPHABETIC-LOWER. The last two are not available in COBOL 74.

There are also two conditions, POSITIVE, NEGATIVE, which may be used with signed numeric data items.

The first class condition, NUMERIC, has already been used in example 5.2, when data was entered into an alphanumeric data item and tested before being moved into a numeric data item; the test will yield true if the item is found to contain only digits. The condition ALPHABETIC will yield true if the item contains only alphabetic characters and spaces. In the following case the test will yield false.

```
MOVE "999999" TO WS-CUST-CODE.
IF WS-CUST-CODE ALPHABETIC ....
```

5.6 Condition Names

A useful facility is available to allow the definition of user-defined names for conditions. This facility may be compared with a boolean function in Pascal (see example 5.6).

Each condition name is declared as a level 88 data item, immediately beneath the data item with which it is connected. Each level 88 declaration includes a VALUE clause associating the name defined with a value or range of values (see example 5.5).

The use of a condition name in the Procedure Division causes the associated data item to be examined to see whether its contents match a value defined in the appropriate level 88. Referring to example 5.5, the effect of

```
IF BURY
```

is the same as

```
IF WS-BRANCH-CODE = "2"
```

It should be noted that condition names may not be used as selection objects in an EVALUATE statement.

Example 5.5 should indicate that this is a useful abstraction facility, which allows us to hide the details of how a condition is implemented and to write code related to the problem being solved. In example 5.5 the use of condition names allows us to write code in the Procedure Division such as

```
IF VALID-BRANCH-CODE
```

which seems more readily understandable and is easier to maintain than alternatives such as

```
IF WS-BRANCH-CODE >= "0" AND <= "5"
IF WS-BRANCH-CODE GREATER THAN "0" AND LESS THAN "6"
IF WS-BRANCH-CODE = "1" OR "2" OR "3" OR "4"
   OR "5" OR "6".
```

```
IDENTIFICATION DIVISION.
PROGRAM-ID.  CONDTNS.

ENVIRONMENT DIVISION.

DATA DIVISION.
WORKING-STORAGE SECTION.
  01  WS-BRANCH-CODE     PIC  X.
      88    VALID-BRANCH-CODE
                          VALUE "1" THROUGH "5".
      88    CROYDON    VALUE "1".
      88    BURY       VALUE "2".
      88    DUDLEY     VALUE "3".
      88    WATFORD    VALUE "4".
      88    DERBY      VALUE "5".
      88    LONDON-AREA
                          VALUE "1"  "4".
      88    MIDLANDS   VALUE "3" "5".

PROCEDURE DIVISION.
PARA-1.
    ACCEPT WS-BRANCH-CODE.
    IF NOT VALID-BRANCH-CODE
        DISPLAY " Invalid Branch code "
    ELSE
      IF LONDON-AREA
            DISPLAY "London area"
      ELSE
          IF MIDLANDS
                DISPLAY "MIDLANDS"
          ELSE
                DISPLAY "BURY BRANCH".
    STOP RUN.
```

Example 5.5 Level 88 Condition names

```
PROGRAM Level88 (Input,Output);
    TYPE QueryType = (Valid, Croydon, Bury, Dudley, Watford,
                      Derby,LondonArea,MidlandsArea);
    VAR BranchCode : Char;
    FUNCTION Branch(Query : QueryType): Boolean;
    BEGIN
        CASE Query OF
        Valid        : Branch := BranchCode = IN ['1'..'5'];
        Croydon      : Branch := BranchCode = '1';
        Bury         : Branch := BranchCode = '2';
        Dudley       : Branch := BranchCode = '3';
        Watford      : Branch := BranchCode = '4';
        Derby        : Branch := BranchCode = '5';
        LondonArea   : Branch := BranchCode = IN ['1','4'];
        MidlandArea  : Branch := BranchCode = IN ['3','5'];
          END
    END; (*Branch Function*)
BEGIN
    Read(BranchCode);
    IF NOT Branch(Valid)
    THEN
        Write('Invalid Branch Code entered')
    ELSE
        IF Branch(LondonArea)
        THEN
            ...
END.
```

Example 5.6 Boolean function equivalent of COBOL condition name

5.7   Selection in COBOL 74

The weaknesses of COBOL 74 have already been mentioned in section 5.2 : although it provides an IF ELSE statement, it provides no direct equivalent of the Case statement, and no statement terminators other than the full stop. It should also be noted that there is no THEN in the IF statement in COBOL 74.

The most serious problem is the lack of statement terminators for the IF ELSE. The full stop denotes the end of the statement that begins with the IF and, therefore, has to be positioned with care.

```
IF  Pence < 1
   THEN
      BEGIN
         Writeln('Error: invalid value for pence entered');
         Writeln('Re-enter pence >');
         Read(Pence)
      END;
         . . . . . . . . . . . . .
```

```
IF  PENCE <  1
   DISPLAY "Error: invalid value for pence entered"
   DISPLAY "Re-enter pence >"
   ACCEPT PENCE.
```

. . . .

Example 5.7 Compound statement in Pascal and COBOL 74

If we were inadvertently to put a full stop at the end of the first indented statement in example 5.7, this would denote the end of the IF statement and the two succeeding indented statements would be executed every time. This is a source of much error.

The lack of a scope delimiter causes difficulties when trying to code a nested IF such as the one in the following outline form in Pascal:

```
IF  condition-1
THEN
   BEGIN
      statement-1;
      IF condition-2
      THEN
         statement-3
      ELSE statement-4;
      statement-5
   END;
```

The Pascal is not explicit, and some confusion may be caused as to the scope of the nested IF (which terminates after statement-4), but it is impossible to produce equivalent in-line code in COBOL 74. The following attempt would not achieve the desired effect:

```
IF   condition-1
     statement-1
     IF condition-2
        statement-3
     ELSE statement-4
     statement-5.
```

Statement-5 would be considered part of the nested IF and would be executed only when condition-2 was false. There is no way in which the programmer can exclude statement-5 from the scope of the nested IF. If the programmer placed a full stop at the end of statement-4 this would terminate the first IF statement as well as the nested IF; statement-5 would then be executed irrespective of condition-1 and condition-2.

This problem has been nicely solved by the introduction of statement terminators into COBOL 85 (see example 5.2 above). One solution in COBOL 74 is to use a PERFORM statement and to place the whole of the nested conditon in a lower-level paragraph:

```
IF   condition-1
     statement-1
     PERFORM LOWER-PARA
     statement-5.
     .........
LOWER-PARA.
     IF condition-2
        statement-3
     ELSE statement-4.
```

There is no Case statement in COBOL 74, but the equivalent logic may be provided using a nested IF, as in example 5.8.

```
IF USER-SELECTION = "1"
   PERFORM NEW-USER
ELSE IF USER-SELECTION  = "2"
        PERFORM   BOOK-RETURN
     ELSE IF USER-SELECTION = "3"
             PERFORM  BOOK-RENEW
          ELSE IF USER-SELECTION = "4"
                  PERFORM  BOOK-LOAN
               ELSE IF USER-SELECTION = "5"
                       PERFORM LIST-BOOKS-OUT
                    ELSE IF USER-SELECTION = "6"
                            PERFORM CLOSE-SYSTEM.
```

Example 5.8 Equivalent of Case statement using nested IF

This is clearly not an ideal solution, and a sequence of simple IF statements might seem more satisfactory, but is less secure because it provides no safeguard against more than one path being executed. There is no protection against the consequences of the variable USER-SELECTION being altered in one of the lower-level procedures. If the user wishes to implement a multi-user selection as a sequence of IF statements, particular care must therefore be taken not to alter the condition within the scope of the complete IF statement.

Study Guide

Make notes on the relational operators available and on the implementation of selection and multiway selection in the COBOL standard used.

Make notes on the use of condition names. What are the advantages of using condition names? Think of examples in which this facility would be useful.

Practical Exercises

1. Users of the 74 standard should transform exercise 5.2 into that standard and compile and execute it.

2. Design, code and test a routine which accepts and validates three values, Quantity, Size and Code from the keyboard. Size may be in range 1 to 10, Quantity in range 10 to 1000, Code in range 25 to 98. Additional invalid combinations are 1) Code 25 to 40 and Size 1 to 5; 2) Quantity < 20 and Code numbers 28, 36, 39. Explanatory error messages should be displayed on the screen. The routine should initially test that each value is numeric.

6 Control Structures 2: Iteration

This chapter introduces the in-line PERFORM and shows how each of the Pascal repetitive statements may be implemented in COBOL 85. The final section shows how they may be implemented in COBOL 74 using the hierarchical PERFORM.

6.1 The In-line PERFORM Statement in COBOL 85

Earlier COBOL standards required iteration to be realised either with IF and GO TO statements or by calling paragraphs using the PERFORM UNTIL and the PERFORM VARYING UNTIL statements (see section 5). COBOL 85 allows each variant of the PERFORM verb to be used to control an in-line sequence of statements terminated by END-PERFORM. PERFORM statements may be nested.

The in-line PERFORM UNTIL is formed as shown below:

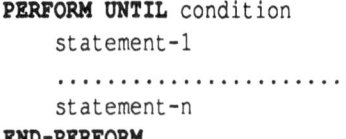

```
PERFORM UNTIL condition
     statement-1
     ......................
     statement-n
END-PERFORM
```

The other variants are constructed in a similar manner. We may now explore the in-line PERFORM further by seeing how it may be used to implement each of the Pascal repetitive statements.

6.2 While Statement

In a While statement the condition is evaluated before execution, so that a While statement executes zero or more times. This feature of the While means that the condition needs to have an initial value before entry, and this is often achieved, as when used to read sequential files, by a read ahead.

We can illustrate the use of the While and the read-ahead with a short routine that validates data entered at the keyboard. In example 6.1 the While takes care of the case when valid data is entered first time, and it also allows a graceful exit from the iteration when valid data is entered after one or more failures.

```
Read(Quantity);
WHILE (Quantity <= 0) OR (Quantity > 1000) DO
BEGIN
   Write ('Error : Quantity out of range. Re-enter >');
   Read(Quantity)
END;
```

Example 6.1 While statement and read ahead in Pascal

We could implement this in COBOL by using the PERFORM UNTIL construct as in example 6.2.

Learners with experience of Pascal often find this difficult to grasp because of confusion with the Pascal Repeat Until, and a common error is to precede the PERFORM UNTIL with a redundant IF statement.

```
. . . . . . . . .
ACCEPT WS-QUANTITY.
PERFORM  UNTIL  WS-QUANTITY > 0
                 AND WS-QUANTITY < 1000
    DISPLAY "ERROR : Quantity out of range;  Re-enter >"
    ACCEPT WS-QUANTITY
END-PERFORM
```

Example 6.2 While equivalent in COBOL 85

The definition of a level 88 condition name

```
01 WS-QUANTITY    PIC 9(4).
   88 VALID-QUANTITY VALUE  1 THROUGH 999.
```

would allow us to produce more elegant code:

```
PERFORM  UNTIL  VALID-QUANTITY
   . . . . . .
END-PERFORM
```

6.3   Repeat Statement

The Repeat statement is used for cases when a loop is required to execute at least once. An example of its use might be in connection with the menu driven library application introduced in chapter 5. We could produce an iterative top level for this application as follows

```
BEGIN (* Main Program *)
    REPEAT
        DisplayMenu;
        AcceptUserChoice;
        ProcessUserChoice;
    UNTIL QuitSelected
END.
```

To implement this in COBOL 85 we would use a PERFORM UNTIL, with an additonal phrase, TEST AFTER, specifying that the condition should be evaluated after each iteration (the default is before). This ensures at least one iteration.

```
..................................
PROCEDURE DIVISION.
CONTROL-PARA.
    PERFORM TEST AFTER UNTIL QUIT
*   a condition name, QUIT, is assumed to be declared in
*   the Working-Storage Section
        PERFORM DISPLAY-MENU
        PERFORM ACCEPT-USER-CHOICE
        PERFORM PROCESS-USER-CHOICE
    END-PERFORM.
    STOP RUN.

DISPLAY-MENU.
* this and succeeding paras are templates only

ACCEPT-USER-CHOICE.

PROCESS-USER-CHOICE.
```

Example 6.3 Repeat equivalent in COBOL 85

It may be noted that the compiler matches the END-PERFORM with the nearest in-line PERFORM. The three nearest PERFORM statements are all performing out-of-line paragraphs and so are ignored, and the first match found is PERFORM TEST AFTER UNTIL QUIT.

6.4   For Statement

The For statement is particularly useful for table handling (see chapter 10), but we can illustrate its use with the following simple example which would display the 2 times table on the screen.

```
FOR Index := 1 TO 12 DO
   Writeln( Index, ' * 2 = ',Index * 2);
```

Example 6.4 FOR statement in Pascal

In COBOL 85 this would be coded as shown in example 6.4.

```
. . . . . . . . . . . . . . . . . . . .
PERFORM TEST AFTER VARYING WS-INDEX FROM
        1 BY 1 UNTIL WS-INDEX = 12
   COMPUTE WS-TOTAL = WS-INDEX * 2
   DISPLAY WS-INDEX "* 2 = " WS-TOTAL
END-PERFORM
. . . . . . . . . . . . . . . . . . . . . .
```

Example 6.5 For statement equivalent in COBOL 85

It should be noted that if the TEST AFTER is omitted then the 12th iteration will not occur, because the default is for the test to be made before each iteration. After the 11th iteration the value of WS-INDEX would be changed to 12, and if the test were made the terminating condition would be true. A less elegant alternative, which is necessary in COBOL 74, is to make the terminating condition > 12.

The PERFORM VARYING is more complex than the Pascal For statement, and the following points should be noted:

1. the programmer may specify any integral initial value and any integral step (except 0), so that if the FROM and BY phrases in example 6.4 were altered to FROM 2 by 2, WS-INDEX would take successive values 2, 4, 6, 8, 10, 12;
2. the condition following UNTIL need not refer to the data-name specified in the VARYING phrase, eg it could in example 6.4 be UNTIL TOTAL = 144; the number of iterations of the statement is therefore not necessarily determinable at entry; the terminating condition could for example be dependent on a value entered at the keyboard;
3. data-names may be used in the FROM and BY phrases.

6.5   Iteration in COBOL 74

The 74 standard does not include in-line PERFORM statements, so that it is necessary to use the out-of-line PERFORM to produce well-structured equivalents for each Pascal iterative statement.

The most important statement used in realising iteration is the PERFORM UNTIL which takes the form

PERFORM para-name **UNTIL** condition

The PERFORM UNTIL logic is like the While statement; the test is made at the beginning and the statement may therefore execute zero times. The Pascal code given in example 6.1 would be coded as shown in example 6.6.

```
. . . . . . . . .
ACCEPT WS-QUANTITY.
PERFORM  INVALID-QUANTITY-PARA
     UNTIL  WS-QUANTITY > 0
           AND WS-QUANTITY < 1000.
. . . . . . . . . . . . . . . .
STOP RUN.
INVALID-QUANTITY-PARA.
    DISPLAY "ERROR : Quantity out of range;  Re-enter >·"
    ACCEPT WS-QUANTITY.
```

Example 6.6 While equivalent using out-of-line Perform

If a user entered a valid quantity initially, then INVALID-QUANTITY-PARA would not be executed.

The code in example 6.6 could be improved by the definition of a level 88 condition name, VALID-QUANTITY, so that the relevant line could be rewritten as

PERFORM INVALID-QUANTITY-PARA **UNTIL** VALID-QUANTITY.

A Repeat statement may be coded by

PERFORM para-name.
PERFORM para-name **UNTIL** condition.

The use of the unconditional PERFORM ensures at least one execution as is the case with the Repeat statement. The example given in example 6.3 above would be coded as shown in example 6.7.

After the first call execution of MAIN-PROCESS the condition QUIT may be true in which case the PERFORM UNTIL executes zero times.

The final Pascal iterative statement, the For statement, and its recommended COBOL near equivalent are given after example 6.7.

```
. . . . . . . . . . . . . . . . . . . . . . . . . . . . . .
PROCEDURE DIVISION.
CONTROL-PARA.
    PERFORM MAIN-PROCESS.
    PERFORM MAIN-PROCESS UNTIL QUIT.
*   a condition name, QUIT, is assumed to be declared
*   in the Working-Storage Section
    STOP RUN.
MAIN-PROCESS.
    PERFORM DISPLAY-MENU.
    PERFORM ACCEPT-USER-CHOICE.
    PERFORM PROCESS-USER-CHOICE.
DISPLAY-MENU.
* this and succeeding paras are templates only

ACCEPT-USER-CHOICE.

PROCESS-USER-CHOICE.
```

Example 6.7 Repeat equivalent in COBOL 74

```
FOR control-statement DO          PERFORM para-name
    statement-1;                  VARYING data-name FROM
                                      initial-value BY step
                                  UNTIL condition.
```

A Pascal For statement which displayed the 2 times table on the screen as shown in example 6.4 would be implemented as follows

```
. . . . . . . . . . . . . . . . . . . .
PERFORM DISPLAY-LINE  VARYING WS-INDEX FROM
    1 BY 1 UNTIL WS-INDEX >12.
STOP RUN.
DISPLAY-LINE.
    COMPUTE WS-TOTAL = WS-INDEX * 2.
    DISPLAY  WS-INDEX "X 2 = " WS-TOTAL.
```

Example 6.8 For statement equivalent using PERFORM VARYING

It should be noted that the terminating condition is > 12. If the condition were = 12 the last iteration would not occur because the test comes at the beginning of each iteration.

Study Suggestions

This chapter has dealt with iteration in COBOL. Readers should ensure that they have notes on the use of each of the PERFORM variants covered in the chapter, both for in-line and out-of-line iteration.

Particular attention should be given to the difference between a Pascal Repeat statement and a COBOL PERFORM UNTIL; the recommended COBOL equivalent of the Repeat statement should be noted for each COBOL standard.

Practical Exercises

1. Amend the final exercise in chapter 5 to require a user to re-input values until valid entries have been made.
2. A program is required to input a sequence of items for an invoice. Each item consists of a Code, Quantity and Price. The invoice total consists of goods total + VAT. The invoice consists of an indeterminate number of items, and the end of the invoice is detected when the user presses carriage return when requested to enter a value into the leading field.

Code this into COBOL using the following pseudo-code design and substituting for each Pascal iterative statement the equivalent COBOL statement:

```
accept code from keyboard
WHILE code <> spaces DO
BEGIN
   REPEAT
      accept Quantity
   UNTIL valid quantity entered
   REPEAT
      accept Price
   UNTIL valid price entered
   add cost of item (quantity * price) to goods total
   accept code from keyboard
END
calculate vat (15%) and add to goods total
display invoice total
```

Part 3

Data
Structures

7 Multi-level Records

This chapter introduces concepts of group and elementary items, shows how multi-level records may be defined and manipulated, and introduces a practical exercise designed to develop understanding of the use of records in COBOL. The use of the REDEFINES clause to define variant records is also introduced in section 4. This may be omitted on a first reading.

7.1 Introduction to Group Items in COBOL

So far in this text we have used elementary data items only, that is to say data items such as

```
01  WS-VAT-RATE   PIC 9(2).
```

which consist of a level number 1, a name and a PICTURE clause. In a typical commercial application it is more usual to group information together into records. We may define a record as a collection of related information, so that a personal record might consist of the following information: name, address, date-of-birth, sex.

COBOL was the first programmming language to provide the facility for declaring records, and has powerful record handling facilities. We will begin by seeing how an instance of the above record would be declared in Pascal (example 7.1).

```
VAR  Person : RECORD
        Name : PACKED ARRAY[1..16] OF Char;
        Address : PACKED ARRAY[1..30] OF Char;
        DateOfBirth : Integer;
        Sex : Char;
     END;
```

Example 7.1 A Pascal Record

The equivalent COBOL record would be declared as in example 7.2.

61

```
WORKING-STORAGE SECTION.
    01 WS-PERSON-REC.
        03 WS-NAME                      PIC X(16).
        03 WS-ADDRESS                   PIC X(30).
        03 WS-DATE-OF-BIRTH             PIC 9(6).
        03  WS-SEX                      PIC X.
```

Example 7.2 Equivalent record in COBOL

In the COBOL declaration the item WS-PERSON-REC, which has no PICTURE clause, is known as a *group item*. The other items, each of which has a PICTURE clause, are known as *elementary items*.

In Pascal it would be possible to copy the contents of the whole record only to another variable of the same type; COBOL provides more flexibility by treating a group item as a sequence of alphanumeric characters. It is possible therefore to move a string of characters, an elementary item, or another record to group item WS-PERSON-REC and to move the whole record to another group or to an elementary item.

The result of the following

```
MOVE SPACES TO WS-PERSON-REC
```

would be to fill each elementary item with spaces. The result of the following

```
MOVE "JONES" TO WS-PERSON-REC
```

would be to store Jones in the first five characters; the remaining characters would be filled with spaces.

We can examine this further by looking at the sequence of instructions in example 7.3.

The first statement initialises WS-PERSON-REC to spaces. The second statement moves the contents of WS-DATE to WS-DATE-OF-BIRTH. It should be noted that this will result in the loss of the two leftmost digits since the receiving field is a numeric field (see chapter 2). If the user enters

```
20011986
```

the value transferred will be

```
011986.
```

The fourth statement will fill the first field of the record with

```
James Robertson
```

```
WORKING-STORAGE SECTION.
    01 WS-PERSON-REC.
        03 WS-NAME                  PIC X(16).
        03 WS-ADDRESS               PIC X(30).
        03 WS-DATE-OF-BIRTH         PIC 9(6).
        03  WS-SEX                  PIC X.
    01 WS-DISPLAY-LINE              PIC X(80).
 * Screen width is 80 characters
    01 WS-DATE                      PIC  X(8).


PROCEDURE DIVISION.
 PARA-1.
     MOVE SPACES TO WS-PERSON-REC.
     ACCEPT WS-DATE.
     MOVE WS-DATE TO WS-DATE-OF-BIRTH.
     MOVE "James Robertson Justice" TO WS-NAME.
     MOVE WS-PERSON-REC TO WS-DISPLAY-LINE.
     DISPLAY WS-DISPLAY-LINE.
 PARA-2.
     MOVE "James Robertson Justice" TO WS-PERSON-REC.
     MOVE WS-ADDRESS TO WS-DISPLAY-LINE.
     DISPLAY WS-DISPLAY-LINE.
     STOP RUN.
```

Example 7.3 Moves involving group items

since the receiving field is alphanumeric, and right truncation occurs. The fifth statement moves the complete record to the elementary item, DISPLAY-LINE, which is then displayed on the screen. The reader should be able to work out what will be displayed on the screen.
In PARA-2 the value

```
James Robertson Justice
```

will be copied, left justified into the group item. The contents of WS-ADDRESS are then displayed on the screen. What are they?

Two points should be noted about group items:

1. The rules for a MOVE are the same as for an alphanumeric item, that is filling takes place from the left, even if the record consists solely of numeric items.

2. Arithmetic operations may not be performed on group items, even if each elementary item is numeric.

7.2   Nested Records

Both Pascal and COBOL allow for records to be nested within each other. We may illustrate this first in Pascal and then in COBOL by amending the above record to make Address and Date-Of-Birth sub-records (see examples 7.4 and 7.5).

```
VAR   Person : RECORD
              Name : PACKED ARRAY[1..16] OF Char;
              Address : RECORD
                       Street :  PACKED ARRAY[1..14] OF Char;
                       Town   :   PACKED ARRAY[1..10] OF Char;
                       Code : PACKED ARRAY[1..6] OF Char;
              END;
              DateOfBirth : RECORD
                           Day: Integer;
                           Month : Integer;
                           Year : Integer;
                 END;
              Sex : Char;
          END;
```

Example 7.4 Nested records in Pascal

```
01 WS-PERSON-REC.
   03 WS-NAME                   PIC X(16).
   03 WS-ADDRESS.
      05 WS-STREET              PIC X(14).
      05 WS-TOWN                PIC X(10).
      05 WS-CODE                PIC X(6).
   03 WS-DATE-OF-BIRTH.
      05 WS-DAY                 PIC 99.
      05 WS-MONTH               PIC 99.
      05 WS-YEAR                PIC 99.
   03   WS-SEX                  PIC X.
```

Example 7.5 Nested records in COBOL

There is a convention of numbering successive levels as 01, 03, 05, 07, 09 as in example 7.5. This makes it easier to alter the record structure by inserting new levels 02, 04 and so on. For example, if it were necessary to amend the record in example 7.5 to create sub-records WS-PERSONAL-DETAILS and WS-COLLEGE-DETAILS, there would be no need to alter the 03 and 05 level records. The alteration would require the insertion of

WS-PERSONAL-DETAILS at level 02 before WS-NAME, and the addition of the sub-record WS-COLLEGE-DETAILS at level 02 after WS-SEX.

7.3 Referencing Fields

The rules for referencing fields are less strict in COBOL than in Pascal. We may manipulate records at any level we choose by simple reference to the name, irrespective of whether the item named is a group or elementary item.

```
MOVE SPACES TO WS-PERSON-REC.
ACCEPT  WS-TOWN.
MOVE "SK42JB" TO WS-CODE.
MOVE ZEROS TO WS-DATE-OF-BIRTH
```

Pascal would require reference to a full pathname for each elementary item, but COBOL requires only that an item is uniquely identified. If a field name is used elsewhere in the program, then the qualifiers IN and OF are available to provide a unique reference. If for example there was another WS-ADDRESS defined elsewhere in the program, we could uniquely identify the one required

```
MOVE SPACES TO WS-ADDRESS IN WS-PERSON-REC.
```

The ability to hyphenate names helps to reduce the need for qualification; for example, to avoid possible duplication WS-ADDRESS could be renamed WS-PERSON-ADDRESS, and it is simpler to do this.

7.4 Variant Records

Inexperienced programmers often have difficulty in understanding the definition of variant records in Pascal, and unless it is well understood it might be better to skip this section on a first reading.

A variant record is a record whose structure varies depending on the contents of a field. We may divide a variant record conceptually into a fixed part and a variant part. We will begin with a simple example of a personal record which has a person's name and, depending on the type of record, a sub-record consisting of either place and date-of-birth or next-of-kin and relationship. To do this in Pascal we would use a tag field and would set up the alternatives as types, as shown in example 7.6.

```
TYPE
      RecType  = (Kin,Birth);
      KinRec = RECORD
        Name:  PACKED ARRAY[1..16] OF Char;
        Relationship : (mother, father ,husband,
                              wife, other);
      END;
      BirthRec = RECORD
        Place:  PACKED ARRAY[1..20] OF Char;
        Date : Integer;
      END;

VAR Person : RECORD
          Name : PACKED ARRAY[1..16] OF Char;
          CASE Transtype :RecType OF
              Kin : ( K: KinRec);
              Birth : (B: BirthRec);
      END;
```

Example 7.6 A variant record in Pascal

The declarations in 7.6 would create the required structure: a record consisting of the person's name followed by one or other of the sub-records.

In COBOL one way of doing this would be to use the REDEFINES as shown in example 7.7. The level 88 condition names are not obligatory, but are useful in this context.

```
01 WS-PERSON-REC.
    03 WS-NAME                 PIC X(16).
    03 WS-REC-TYPE             PIC X.
        88 KIN-REC    VALUE "K".
        88 BIRTH-REC  VALUE "B".
    03 WS-BIRTH-REC.
        05  WS-PLACE           PIC X(20).
        05  WS-DATE            PIC 9(6).
    03 WS-KIN-REC  REDEFINES WS-BIRTH-REC.
        05  WS-NAME            PIC X(16).
        05  WS-RELATION        PIC X.
            88 MOTHER    VALUE "M".
            88 FATHER    VALUE "F".
            88 HUSBAND   VALUE "H"
            88 WIFE      VALUE "W".
            88 OTHERS    VALUE "O".
```

Example 7.7 REDEFINES used to define variant record

The REDEFINES produces two views on the same memory space: if the variant part, WS-BIRTH-REC contained the following:

|K|I|N|G|S|T|O|N| - |O|N| - |T|H|A|M|E|S| | | |0|3|0|4|6|1|

The contents of each field would be as follows:

WS-PLACE

|K|I|N|G|S|T|O|N| - |O|N| - |T|H|A|M|E|S| | | |

WS-DATE

|0|3|0|4|6|1|

WS-NAME

|K|I|N|G|S|T|O|N| - |O|N| - |T|H|A|M|

WS-RELATION

|E|

WS-KIN-REC

|K|I|N|G|S|T|O|N| - |O|N| - |T|H|A|M|E|

It should be clear that in this particular case viewing the variant part as WS-KIN-REC will give erroneous results. To guard against this the WS-REC-TYPE field in the fixed part of the record would be used by the programmer to check whether to view the variant part as WS-PLACE followed by WS-DATE, or alternatively as WS-NAME followed by WS-RELATION. In the above example WS-REC-TYPE should contain 'B' since the record held in the variant part is clearly WS-BIRTH-REC and not WS-KIN-REC. It is the responsibility of the programmer to make this check, the system would not detect any error if it was omitted, nor if an incorrect value was entered in WS-REC-TYPE.

It should be noted that a data item may only be redefined by another item with the same level number.

Further coverage of the REDEFINES clause occurs in chapter 10. An alternative way of defining variant records for sequential files is shown in chapter 8 (section 8.5 on multi-record files).

Study Suggestion

This chapter has introduced the concept of group items in COBOL and has shown how group items may be declared and manipulated.

You are recommended to make notes on the rules for moving group items, and to note the rules for referencing data items, including the use of qualifiers.

Practical Exercise

It should be apparent that a multi-level record may be represented as a tree structure. A record represented in this way can readily be converted into a COBOL declaration, beginning with the root which becomes the level 1 group item. This may be illustrated with the following example of a Student-Record.

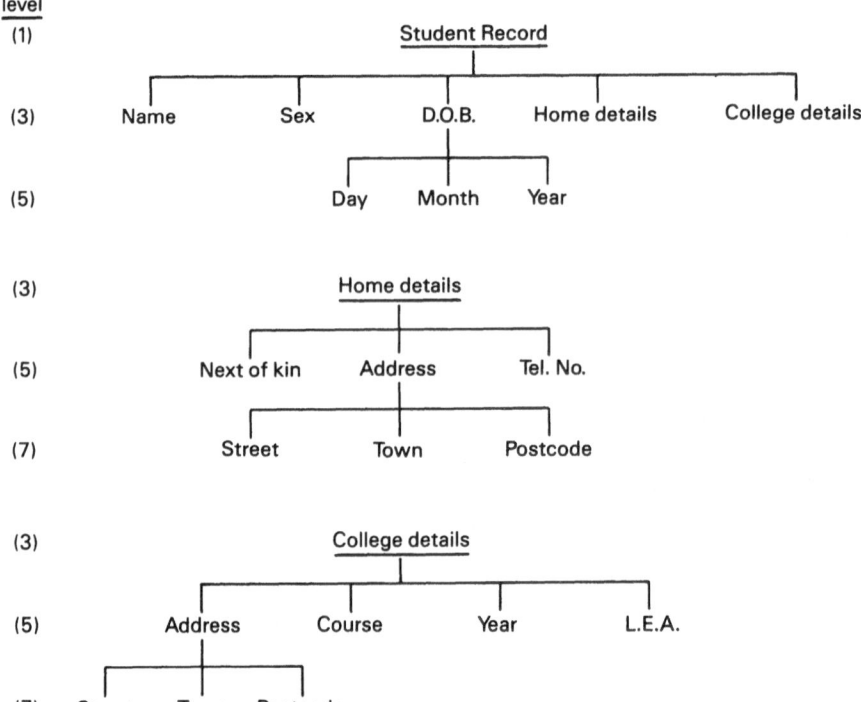

The record as denoted on the tree structure maps easily on to a COBOL data definition. Student-record is at level 01, at level 03 there are five fields (two are elementary and three are grouped), so that the record will have in outline the following structure:

```
Student-Record
        Name
        Sex
        DateOfBirth
          Day
          Month
          Year
        Home details
          Next of kin
          Address
                  Street
                  Town
                  Postcode
          Tel. No.
      College details
          Address
                  Street
                  Town
                  Postcode
          Course
          Year
          Local Education Authority.
```

It is now a trivial if lengthy matter to create a COBOL record. The only decisions that are left are the types and sizes of the elementary fields.

It is wise to use hyphenated names to avoid using reserved words (DAY is a reserved word) and to provide unique names for each item.

The record should first be written on paper (on a COBOL coding sheet if available), and then entered into the Working-Storage Section of a previously compiled template.

The program with the record description should then be recompiled and any compilation errors removed.

When the program has compiled successfully, the Procedure Division should be amended to allow data for the record to be entered from the keyboard. It should be noted that data may be entered into group or elementary items. We shall use the program to create a sequential file in chapter 8.

8 Sequential Files

This chapter introduces the facilities available for processing sequential files, and shows how the Environment, Data and Procedure Divisions are coded in order to set up and process sequential files. The chapter concludes with a practical exercise in which the program begun in chapter 7 is developed to allow the creation of a sequential file from the keyboard.

8.1 Introduction to Sequential Files

A sequential or serial file consists of a sequence of data items, terminated by an end of file marker, and stored on some non-volatile medium such as disk or magnetic tape.

Pascal allows us to declare serial files and process them as follows:

i) Open a file for reading and, beginning with the first item, transfer items in sequence from the file into main memory.

ii) Open a file for writing, the effect of which is to create a new, empty file, and to append items to the file.

These standard facilities are available in COBOL and are useful for file applications in which a relatively high percentage of items require processing.

COBOL provides additional, less-used facilities files which allow us to

iii) Append items to an existing sequential file;

iv) Open a sequential file for simultaneous reading, writing and updating items in place.

Before we investigate the COBOL facilities further it may help to remind ourselves how we would set up and open a file in Pascal.

The Pascal program fragment in example 8.1 would declare a serial file of type PersonRec, open it for reading, and transfer the first record into the associated file buffer.

The COBOL equivalent requires entries in the Environment, Data and Procedure Divisions. The entry in the Procedure Division is comparable to that in the statement part of the Pascal program, but the Environment and Data Division entries are difficult to relate to what appear to be the simpler entries needed in Pascal.

```
PROGRAM FileHandler(Input,Output,Data);
TYPE PersonRec : RECORD
        Name : PACKED ARRAY[1..20] OF Char;
        Address : PACKED ARRAY[1..30] OF Char;
        DateOfBirth : Integer;
        Sex : Char;
     END;


VAR  Data : FILE OF PersonRec;

BEGIN
   Reset(DATA);
   .......
END.
```

Example 8.1 Declaring and opening a file for reading in Pascal

8.2   Selection of a File in the Environment Division

This allows association of a filename with a peripheral device and indicates what type of file is to be created, and how the file may be accessed.

```
ENVIRONMENT DIVISION.
INPUT-OUTPUT SECTION.
FILE-CONTROL.
    SELECT    DATA-FILE
    ASSIGN TO    device-name
    ORGANIZATION IS SEQUENTIAL
    ACCESS MODE IS SEQUENTIAL.
```

Example 8.2 Environment Division entry for a sequential file

Each file that is used must have an appropriate SELECT statement in the File-Control paragraph.

The name given to the file, DATA-FILE in example 7.1, is programmer-defined, and is used whenever the file is referred to elsewhere in the program.

The installation manual should be consulted for the device-name. Readers will find a variety of options, but usually DISK and PRINTER will be the available options. There will usually be some facility for associating the internal file-name declared in the SELECT clause with a different external file-name. Some implementors provide an optional VALUE OF FILE-ID clause in the File Description in the Data Division. This allows the file to be assigned either to a non-numeric literal or a to data-name. Logically, it might seem more appropriately included in the Environment Division.

The ORGANIZATION and ACCESS clauses specify the logical structure of a file and how the record may be addressed. These clauses are optional for sequential files, since the default is for sequential access and organisation. It is good practice to put them in for documentation purposes. In some systems the programmer may need to specify whether the file is organised into records or lines.

A number of other options are available, but for learning purposes the above example is adequate.

8.3   File Description in the Data Division

For each file selected there must be a description in the Data Division(see example 8.3).

```
DATA DIVISION.
FILE SECTION.
FD   DATA.
  01 PERSON-REC.
     03 NAME              PIC X(20).
     03 ADDRESS           PIC X(30).
     03 DATE-OF-BIRTH     PIC 9(6).
     03 SEX               PIC X.
```

Example 8.3 File Section entry for a file

The FD (File Description) sentence should begin in area A. The file name must match the file name selected in the Environment Division. There are a number of clauses which may be used after the file name in the FD statement, but in the 85 standard all are optional, although some implementations may require their use.

Each file description must contain a description of the record or records contained on the file. Records in the File Section are declared in the same way as in the Working-Storage Section except that a VALUE clause may not be used unless it is part of a level 88 item. Level number 01 or 1 must begin in area A.

The records declared in the File Section may be used in the same way as those declared in the Working-Storage Section, but their main purpose is to act as file buffers. When a READ is executed, data is transferred from the file into its record area. When a WRITE executed the data currently stored in the record area is written to the appropriate file, and after the execution of the WRITE statement it is no longer available in the record area.

8.4   File Processing Entries in the Procedure Division

Each file selected in the Environment Division must be opened in the Procedure Division. Example 8.4 shows how to open the file defined in previous examples and how to transfer the first record from the file into the record area defined in the File Section.

```
PROCEDURE DIVISION.
PARA-1.
   OPEN  INPUT  DATA-FILE.
   READ DATA-FILE
      AT END
         MOVE "E" TO WS-END-OF-DATA-FILE.
   . . . . . . . . . . . . . .
```

Example 8.4 Opening and reading from a sequential file

The first statement in example 8.4 opens the file for reading. If the file were to be opened for writing the form would be

OPEN OUTPUT DATA-FILE.

More than one file name may be specified after the OPEN verb, so that the OPEN sentence for a sequential file update program with two input files, Old-Master and Transaction-File, would be written as follows:

OPEN INPUT OLD-MASTER   TRANSACTION-FILE.

The READ verb requires an AT END clause for sequential file reading. This defines the action to be taken if the end of the file is reached. A sensible action is to set a status variable as in example 8.4 above. This status variable should be declared and initialised in Working-Storage, and should preferably include a condition name (level 88). (See example 8.5).

```
WORKING-STORAGE SECTION.
   01 WS-END-OF-DATA-FILE           PIC  X
                 VALUE "N".
         88  END-OF-DATA-FILE       VALUE "E"
```

Example 8.5 End-of-file status variable with condition name

COBOL 85 provides a statement terminator for the READ verb and also a NOT AT END phrase. This may be a useful addition when there are certain operations which may only be done when a record is successfully read as shown in example 8.6.

```
PROCEDURE DIVISION.
PARA-1.
    OPEN  INPUT  DATA-FILE.
    READ DATA-FILE
      AT END
        MOVE "E" TO WS-END-OF-DATA-FILE
      NOT AT END
        ADD 1 TO RECORD-COUNT
    END-READ
        . . . . . . . . . . . . .
```

Example 8.6 Use of END-READ and NOT AT END, COBOL 85

Example 8.6 assumes an elementary numeric item, RECORD-COUNT, declared in the Working-Storage Section.

Over-use of the NOT AT END could lead to lazy programming, and poor structuring; the processing of a record should be kept logically distinct from the reading of a record. The use of a read ahead and a PERFORM UNTIL should minimise the need for the NOT AT END phrase, as is shown in example 8.7.

```
PROCEDURE DIVISION.
PARA-1.
    OPEN  INPUT  DATA
    READ DATA
      AT END
        MOVE "E" TO WS-END-OF-DATA-FILE.
    PERFORM UNTIL END-OF-DATA-FILE OR REC-FOUND
      ADD 1 TO RECORD-COUNT
      DISPLAY PERSON-REC
      READ DATA
        AT END
        MOVE "E" TO WS-END-OF-DATA-FILE
      END-READ.
    END-PERFORM.
        . . . . . . . . . .
```

Example 8.7 Read Ahead and in-line PERFORM UNTIL, COBOL 85

Users of COBOL 74 should note that example 8.7 needs the following modification:
i) the in-line PERFORM should be converted to an out-of-line PERFORM;
ii) the END-READ and END-PERFORM should be removed;
iii) the statements from ADD onwards should be placed in a lower-level paragraph.

The verb WRITE is used to transfer data to a file that has been opened for output.

```
PROCEDURE DIVISION.
PARA-1.
       OPEN   OUTPUT  DATA-FILE.
       MOVE "A.R. JONES" TO NAME.
       MOVE "30 High St Saxmundham" TO ADDRESS.
       MOVE  121239 TO DATE-OF-BIRTH.
       MOVE "M" TO SEX.
*  Previous code moves information into record area
       WRITE PERSON-REC.
       CLOSE DATA-FILE.
       STOP RUN
```

Example 8.8 Writing a single record to a sequential file

Example 8.8 shows how a single record could be written to the file. It assumes the same Environment and Data Division entries shown in earlier examples. The effect of course would be to delete any existing file by the same name and to create a new file containing the one record.

It should be noted that whereas the READ verb requires a *file name*, the WRITE verb requires a *record name* to be specified. This is a source of confusion to beginners.

The WRITE also has a statement terminator, and certain optional features useful in writing to a printer or to a report file. These will be covered later.

Each file selected must also be closed; this may be done before the program terminates, as in example 8.8. The CLOSE verb may be followed by a list of all the files used, irrespective of whether they have been opened for reading or writing.

```
CLOSE  filename    filename ...
```

8.5 Appending Records to an Existing File

In Pascal if we wish to add records to an existing file we must open the existing file for reading, open a new file for writing, copy the contents of the existing file to the new file, and then add records to the new file. COBOL provides a facility which allows us to append records to an existing file. To do so we must declare a sequential file as previously, and use the EXTEND option when the file is opened:

```
OPEN   EXTEND   filename  filename ...
```

this allows us to use the WRITE statement to append records to the file.

8.6   Updating a Sequential File in Place

Normally a sequential file update involves amendments to existing records, insertion of new records, and deletion of records. If these operations are required then it is necessary to perform a father–son update by using a transaction file and a master file as input, and then processing the two together to produce a new master file. If however, all that is required is the amendment of existing records, it is possible in COBOL to update records on a sequential file in place. To do this it is necessary to declare the sequential file in the same way as in previous examples, and to open it for input and output:

```
OPEN    I-O     filename    filename..
```

In example 8.9 a single record in a file is updated in place, and the processing is terminated when that record has been updated. It would of course be inefficient to select sequential file organisation for such a problem, but it is given purely as a simple example.

```
PROCEDURE DIVISION.
PARA-1.
    OPEN  I-O  DATA-FILE.
    READ DATA-FILE
      AT END
         MOVE "E" TO WS-END-OF-DATA-FILE
         DISPLAY "Record not found"
    END-READ
    PERFORM UNTIL END-OF-DATA-FILE OR RECORD-FOUND
       IF NAME = "A.R.JONES"
         THEN
            MOVE 220352 TO DATE-OF-BIRTH
            REWRITE PERSON-REC
            MOVE "Y" TO WS-RECORD-FOUND
         ELSE
            READ DATA-FILE
             AT END
                MOVE "E" TO WS-END-OF-DATA-FILE
                DISPLAY "Record not found"
            END-READ
       END-IF
    END-PERFORM
    CLOSE DATA-FILE.
    STOP RUN.
```

Example 8.9 Updating in place on a sequential file, COBOL 85

Example 8.9 assumes another variable WS-RECORD-FOUND with a level 88 data name, RECORD-FOUND, which is set when the record to be amended has been rewritten. The programmer should in such situations resist the temptation to pretend that end-of-file has been reached and alter the condition of the end of file variable.

The COBOL 74 coding for the example in 8.9 is given in example 8.10.

```
PROCEDURE DIVISION.
PARA-1.
    OPEN  I-O  DATA-FILE.
    READ DATA-FILE
      AT END
        MOVE "E" TO WS-END-OF-DATA-FILE
        DISPLAY "Record not found".
    PERFORM UPDATE-REC
      UNTIL END-OF-DATA-FILE OR RECORD-FOUND.
    CLOSE DATA-FILE.
    STOP RUN.
UPDATE-REC.
    IF NAME = "A.R.JONES"
        MOVE 220352 TO DATE-OF-BIRTH
        REWRITE PERSON-REC
        MOVE "Y" TO WS-RECORD-FOUND.
    ELSE
        READ DATA-FILE
          AT END
            MOVE "E" TO WS-END-OF-DATA-FILE
            DISPLAY "Record not found".
    .................
```

Example 8.10 Updating in place on a sequential file, COBOL 74

8.7 Multi-Record Files

Sometimes we require a file which has a number of differing record structures. This could be done using REDEFINES (as shown in chapter 7), but we may simply provide alternative record descriptions.

If, for example, we wish to use a file which handles batches of records we may wish to have a batch header record which consists of batch-number, date, code of checker, number in batch. We could declare the file and the records as shown in example 8.11.

```
DATA DIVISION.
FILE SECTION.
FD  DATA-FILE.
    01 PERSON-REC.
        03 REC-TYPE        PIC X.
            88 BATCH-HEADER-REC
                           VALUE "H".
            88 DATA-REC VALUE "D".
        03 NAME            PIC X(20).
        03 ADDRESS         PIC X(30).
        03 DATE-OF-BIRTH   PIC 9(6).
        03 SEX             PIC X.
    01 HEADER-REC.
        03 REC-TYPE        PIC X.
        03 CHECKER         PIC XX.
        03 DATE-CHECKED    PIC X(6).
        03 NUMBER-IN-BATCH PIC 99.

PROCEDURE DIVISION.
PARA-1.
            . . . . . .
        IF BATCH-HEADER-REC
            PERFORM PROCESS-BATCH
        ELSE
            PERFORM PROCESS-DATA
            . . . . . . . . . .
        STOP RUN


PROCESS-BATCH.


PROCESS-DATA.
```

Example 8.11 Alternative record descriptions for a file

It should be noted that each record has one field in common which may be checked to determine the type of record read and to call the appropriate paragraph to process the record. It should be remembered that when a record is written COBOL requires the record name to be specified, so that the system knows the length of record to write; when the file is read, whatever record is next in sequence is transferred into the memory area shared by the alternative records; it is up to the programmer to establish what view to take of that memory area, by checking the contents of REC-TYPE. It should be noted that the level 88 conditions declared in example 8.11 may be used when a header record has been read, even though they have been included in the PERSON-REC declaration. This is because the header and data records simply provide different views of the same memory area.

Practical Exercise

In the previous chapter an exercise was begun which allowed a multi-level student-record to be accepted from the keyboard. We may now amend this program to allow a sequence of records to be read in this way and written to a file. The code required to declare, open and write to the file has already been covered in this chapter. The program will require a loop structure, and a mechanism to allow the user to terminate input. One solution is to use the first field in the record as a terminator, and to combine this with a read-ahead technique. The design for this in pseudo code will be

```
Open file for output;
Read first field from keyboard;
WHILE first field <> spaces DO
  Read record body from keyboard;
  Write record to file
  Read first field from keyboard
END;
Close file
```

We may transform the While loop structure into a PERFORM UNTIL as shown in chapter 6 and write an outline Procedure Division, as in example 8.12.

```
PROCEDURE DIVISION.
CONTROL-PARA.
    OPEN OUTPUT STUDENT-FILE.
    ACCEPT WS-NAME.
    PERFORM MAIN-PROCESS UNTIL WS-NAME = SPACES.
    CLOSE STUDENT-FILE.
    STOP RUN.


MAIN-PROCESS.
    PERFORM ACCEPT-REC-BODY.
    MOVE WS-STUDENT-REC TO STUDENT-REC.
    WRITE STUDENT-REC.
    ACCEPT WS-NAME.
ACCEPT-REC-BODY.
    . . . . . . . . . . . . . . . . . .
```

Example 8.12 Creating sequential file from keyboard input

The solution in example 8.12 assumes that keyboard input is into a record in Working-Storage, WS-STUDENT-REC, which is then moved to a record of identical size in the File Section. There is no need for the complete record to be specified in full in the File Section. The simplest solution is to declare STUDENT-REC as an elementary field with a length equal to the combined total of all the elementary fields in WS-STUDENT-REC.

It is also possible to avoid the move preceding the write sentence by using an alternative form of the write

```
WRITE STUDENT-REC FROM WS-STUDENT-REC.
```

A similar alternative for the READ, the READ INTO allows a record to be transferred without a move into either a record in the Working-Storage Section or another file record area if required.

Having completed the above program we may now amend the design to enable us to read back the file stored and to display each record in turn on the screen:

```
Open student file for input;
Read record from file;
WHILE NOT end of student file  DO
  Display record on  screen
  Read keyboard
  Read record from file
END;
Display no-more-records-message on screen
Close file
```

The use of the read ahead should again be noted. The keyboard is read after each record display to allow a user to indicate when the next record is to be displayed on the screen.

You may now wish to complete this exercise using the previous program as an example. Recall that if a sequential file is to be read, a Working-Storage data item will be required to deal with the end-of-file (see examples 8.5 and 8.6).

9   Data Editing and Report Writing

This chapter introduces COBOL's facilities for producing edited output and shows how these facilities may be used to set up report lines in the Working-Storage Section. The chapter concludes with an extended example and practical exercise involving writing of a program to produce a report from a sequential file.

9.1   Edited Data

The concept of edited data is one which is unknown in Pascal. For example, if we wished to write a column of real numbers, right-aligned with a preceding currency sign, such as

```
£123.45
  £0.98
 £16.75
```

we would need to adjust the field-width of the currency sign character according to the number of digits required by the number, which would not be a simple matter to program.

If we wished to produce output such as

```
  £123,456.78
     £367.00
   £1,234.08
£1,167,890.00
```

we would find equal if not greater difficulty.

The ability to produce output in this way is invaluable for producing reports, and COBOL has included standard facilities for producing edited output. For example, to solve the first problem we could set up an *edited numeric field*

```
01  WS-OUTPUT-COST        PIC £££9.99.
```

The effect of moving 123.45 to this field and then displaying or writing it to a file would be to produce output as required above. Similarly, for the output requiring the commas as separators we could set up another edited field

    01   WS-OUTPUT-TOTAL-COST **PIC** ££,£££,££9.99.

which would behave in the way required; that is, it would produce right-aligned output with a floating currency sign and commas as appropriate.

A number of special characters may be inserted in picture clauses to produce output for reports and screen display. The most important of these characters are

.   decimal point – used for numeric display
,   comma (used especially with large numbers, eg 1,000,000)
Z   zero suppression
£(or $)   currency sign, used either as leftmost character or as floating sign to suppress leading zeros
- +   signs, used either as single characters (leading or trailing) or as floating signs

It should be emphasised that edited fields set up with special characters, including the decimal point, are for display purposes only and the compiler will reject any attempt to use them for calculation purposes.

We may illustrate the behaviour of the floating zero suppression character with the table shown in example 9.1.

```
-------------------------------------------------------------------
Source PIC     Source Value    Display PIC       Value Displayed

 99999V99        0001234        ZZZZ9.99                   12.34
 99999V99        1000001        ZZZZ9.99                10000.01
 99999V99        0000000        ZZZZZ.ZZ
 99999V99        0000001        ZZZZZ.ZZ                     .01
-------------------------------------------------------------------
```

Example 9.1 Editing using zero suppression

In the first example given in example 9.1 the result of moving 0001234 from a numeric field with picture 99999V99 to a display data item with the picture ZZZZ9.99 would be to produce a display value of 12.34; if 00000.00 were moved to the same display field the result would be 0.00.

It should be noted that zero suppression may be used after the decimal point only if all positions to the left of the point are also suppressed. It should also be noted that the system will automatically align an item moved around the decimal point.

Example 9.2 shows the behaviour of the currency sign and commas.

Source PIC	Source Value	Display PIC	Value Displayed
99999v99	0001234	£££££9.99	£12.34
99999v99	0000000	£££££££.££	
99999v99	0000006	£££££££.££	£0.06
99999v99	0001234	£99,999.99	£00,012.34
99999v99	0123456	£££,£££.99	£1,234.56

Example 9.2. Editing using currency sign and commas

When used as a floating character the currency sign acts similarly to the zero suppression character - it suppresses leading zeros and places the currency sign in the position of the rightmost suppressed zero.

In the penultimate line in example 9.2 the currency sign is used as a fixed character, and will always be displayed in the same position. The currency sign may not be combined with zero suppression..

Finally, as the table in example 9.3 shows the use of signs as floating and fixed characters.

Source PIC	Source Value	Display PIC	Value Displayed
S99999v99	-0001101	-----9.99	-11.01
S99999v99	+0001001	-----9.99	10.01
S99999v99	-0020001	+++++9.99	-200.01
S99999v99	+0000401	+++++9.99	+4.01
S99999v99	-0020001	+99999.99	-00200.01
S99999v99	+0000401	+99999.99	+00004.01
S99999v99	+1000001	-99999.99	10000.01
S99999v99	-1000001	-99999.99	-10000.01
S99999V99	-1000001	99999.99+	10000.01-

Example 9.3 Signs used as editing characters

As shown in example 9.3 the sign characters may be used either as floating characters or as fixed characters. When used as floating characters they act as zero suppression characters in the same way as the Z and the currency sign.

It should be noted that the only way to ensure that a + sign is displayed is to use the + character, whereas a − sign will be displayed whether a + or - editing character is used. The sign characters may also be used as trailing characters, as shown in the last line of example 9.3.

9.2 Setting up Display Records in the Working-Storage Section

We frequently need to interrogate files to produce a report in which data is output in a readable, attractive form, with columns aligned, zeros suppressed, currency signs printed and units of one thousand separated by commas. An important element of such a task is to analyse the output requirements and to set up the necessary data items in Working-Storage.

To illustrate this, let us suppose that we are required to interrogate a customer file to produce a report on all customers with outstanding accounts. Details about the customer file are given in section 9.4. The report is to consist of an unknown number of pages; each page is to be set out as shown in example 9.4. There may be up to 20 detail lines on a page. On the first page there will be no brought-forward line, on the last page there will be no carried-forward line, but there will be a line giving the overall total. Lines of text other than the total lines are double spaced.

It is advisable to plan the report layout on a squared layout chart, so that columns can be correctly positioned. Specifications for report programs will usually contain such a chart.

```
------------------------------------------------------------------
                        R. Canyon Associates

                   Accounts Outstanding       15/12/87     Page 2

Name                    Address                             Amount
                   _____
A.R. Jones              12, Derby Road, Wangford            £12.15

L.N. Smith              23 Daventry Crescent, Heaton Chapel £101.25

J.R.  Beans             9, The Gables, Baldock            £1,192.34

L.F.  Williams          6, Leary Crescent, Cringle        £2,079.27

N.L. Toquet             Braemar, Rochdale Rd, Middleton     £154.32

..............          ...................................  ........

     Total                                                 £996.71
     Brought forward from previous page                   £1987.07
     Carried forward                                      £2983.78
------------------------------------------------------------------
```

Example 9.4 Specimen page from overdue accounts report

We may identify nine different lines that will be required for the report: three header lines, four footers, one line of underscore characters, which appears twice, and one detail line, which appears up to 20 times. The four footers are required because the last page has a different final line.

The approach that we shall follow is to set up a suitable data item for each of these lines in the Working-Storage Section. An initial identification of each field is given in example 9.5.

```
WORKING-STORAGE SECTION.
    01  WS-REPORT-OUTPUT.
* This record is incomplete and will not compile
        03  WS-HEADER-1.
        03  WS-HEADER-2.

        03  WS-HEADER-3.

        03  WS-LINE.
            05  FILLER                  PIC X(10)
                VALUE SPACES.
            05  FILLER                  PIC X(100)
                VALUE ALL "_".

        03  WS-DETAIL-LINE.

        03  WS-PAGE-TOTAL-LINE.

        03  WS-BROUGHT-FORWARD-LINE.

        03  WS-CARRIED-FORWARD-LINE.

        03  WS-OVERALL-TOTAL-LINE.
```

Example 9.5 Output fields required

In example 9.5 the only complete item is WS-LINE. This item contains two elementary fields each of which has been defined using the reserved word FILLER. This is used for declaring an elementary item whose value will not change and whose name will not be referred to in the Procedure Division. When we write WS-LINE the characters written will be 10 spaces followed by a line 100 characters wide; this will leave a margin on the right-hand side.

Without a layout chart it is difficult to complete the remaining declarations, but we can outline the code required for a few, and will leave decisions on some picture sizes to the reader.

The first header would, like WS-LINE, consist of two elementary fields initialised using FILLER (see example 9.6).

```
03  WS-HEADER-1.
    05  FILLER                    PIC X(50)
            VALUE SPACES.
    05  FILLER                    PIC X(20)
            VALUE  "R. Canyon Associates".
```

Example 9.6 Declaration of the first header line

The second header would be more complex, since in addition to various FILLER items it requires two variable data items, WS-DATE and WS-PAGE-NO (see example 9.7).

```
03 WS-HEADER-2.
    05  FILLER        PIC X( )
            VALUE SPACES.
    05  FILLER        PIC X(20)
            VALUE "Accounts Outstanding".
    05  FILLER        PIC X( )
            VALUE SPACES.
    05  WS-DATE       PIC 99/99/99.
    05  FILLER    PIC X( )
            VALUE SPACES.
    05  FILLER        PIC X(4)
            VALUE "Page".
    05  WS-PAGE-NO    PIC 99
            VALUE ZEROS.
```

Example 9.7 Declaration of second header line

The slash in the WS-DATE picture clause is an additional editing character which will separate day, month and year; the date will be accepted from the computer into a numeric data item and then moved to the display field, WS-DATE. WS-PAGE-NO has been given an initial-value of 0; it will be incremented as each new page is written.

The detail line will consist of three variable data items, WS-DETAIL-NAME, WS-DETAIL-ADDRESS and WS-DETAIL-AMOUNT, each of which will be moved from the input file to the appropriate item in WS-DETAIL-LINE. It also consists of three FILLER fields to provide appropriate margin and spacing between output fields.

```
03 WS-DETAIL-LINE.
    05   FILLER                          PIC X()
              VALUE SPACES.
    05   WS-DETAIL-NAME                   PIC  X(20).
    05   FILLER                          PIC X()
              VALUE SPACES.
    05   WS-DETAIL-ADDRESS                PIC X(30).
    05   FILLER                          PIC X()
              VALUE SPACES.
    05   WS-DETAIL-AMOUNT                 PIC £££,££9.99.
```

Example 9.8 Detail line declaration

Suggested Exercise

Using suitable squared paper design a layout for the above report and complete the Working-Storage coding. Enter into a previously compiled template, compile the program and remove all compilation errors.

9.3   Writing Display Records to a Report File

To write the report we need to select and describe an output file as shown in chapter 8. The file should be described as shown in example 9.9. It should be noted that the record associated with the file is in the example declared as an elementary item; this is in line with our strategy of assembling the report lines in Working-Storage and moving data to the output record as required. The picture field of the output record, currently left incomplete, should be set to the number of characters output by the printer.

```
DATA DIVISION.
FILE SECTION.
FD  REPORT-FILE.
    01  PRINT-LINE                PIC X( ).
```

Example 9.9 Report file record description

In the Procedure Division we then open the file for output. Each detail line of the report is assembled in the appropriate place in Working-Storage and may then as required be written to the report file. We have two alternatives, either

```
MOVE WS-DETAIL-LINE TO PRINT-LINE.
WRITE PRINT-LINE.
```

or we use the write from

```
WRITE PRINT-LINE FROM WS-DETAIL-LINE.
```

We may obtain double spacing of lines by

```
WRITE PRINT-LINE AFTER 2 LINES.
```

We may force a new page by the following

```
WRITE PRINT-LINE AFTER PAGE.
```

To write all the headings required at the start of the page we could produce a paragraph as shown in example 9.10. This paragraph forces a new page, and then writes each heading, double spaced.

```
            . . . . . . . . . . . .
        WRITE-HEADINGS.
            MOVE SPACES TO PRINT-LINE.
            WRITE PRINT-LINE AFTER PAGE.
            WRITE PRINT-LINE FROM WS-HEADER-1.
            WRITE PRINT-LINE FROM WS-HEADER-2 AFTER 2.
            WRITE PRINT-LINE FROM WS-HEADER-3 AFTER 2.
```

Example 9.10 Printing page headings

A similar paragraph could be produced for the page footers. The main body of the page would be a loop structure, terminated either at the end of the input file or when 20 records have been output to the page.

9.4 Designing the Report Writing Program

The customer file is a sequential file with the following record:

```
01 CUSTOMER-REC.
    03 CUST-NAME                PIC X(20).
    03 CUST-ADDRESS             PIC X(30).
    03 AMOUNT-OUTSTANDING       PIC 999V99.
```

All customers with a non-zero amount outstanding are to be listed in the report. Whenever a non-zero amount is read the detail line is prepared and then written to the report file as shown in the preceding section.

The top level of the program may be defined as follows

```
Open files;
Set CarriedForwardTotal to Zero;
Read Customer-file;
WHILE NOT EndOfCustomerFile DO
    ProducePage;
Close files
```

The data item CarriedForwardTotal will be used to keep a running total of the amount shown in the report; it may be initialised in the Working-Storage Section rather than in the Procedure Division.

ProducePage can be refined as follows:

```
PROCEDURE ProducePage;

BEGIN
    Increment PageNo
    Set PageTotal to Zero
    Set LineCount to 1
    WriteHeadings
    WHILE LineCount <= 20 AND NOT EndOfCustomerFile DO
        ProcessCustomerRec;
        Move OverallTotal to BroughtForwardTotal;
        Add PageTotal to CarriedForwardTotal;
        WriteFooter
END; (*ProducePage*)
```

WriteHeadings is a simple sequence which writes each header and a line in turn. Code for this has already been given in example 9.10.

ProcessCustomerRec can be refined as follows:

```
PROCEDURE ProcessCustomerRec;
BEGIN
    IF AmountOutstanding > Zero
        THEN
            BEGIN
                Write detail line;
                Add AmountOutstanding to PageTotal;
                Increment LineCount
            END;
    Read CustomerFile
END; (*ProcessCustomerRec*)
```

WriteFooters can be refined as

```
PROCEDURE WriteFooters;
BEGIN
        Write Line
        Write PageTotalLine
        IF PageNo > 1
           THEN Write BroughtForwardTotalLine
        IF NOT EndOfCustomerFile
           THEN Write CarriedForwardTotalLine
        ELSE
           BEGIN
               Move CarriedForwardTotal to OverallTotal
               Write OverallTotalLine
           END
END; (*WriteFooters*)
```

This design can now be coded into COBOL; we shall produce an outline only, leaving the reader to complete the program as an exercise.

```
PROCEDURE DIVISION.
CONTROL-PARA.
        ..............
        PERFORM PRODUCE-PAGE UNTIL END-OF-CUSTOMER-FILE.
* A level 88 declaration END-OF-CUSTOMER-FILE is assumed
        ..............
        STOP RUN.

PRODUCE-PAGE.
        ..............
        PERFORM PROCESS-CUSTOMER-REC UNTIL
           WS-LINE-COUNT > 20 OR END-OF-CUSTOMER-FILE.
        ............

PROCESS-CUSTOMER-REC.
        ..............

WRITE-HEADINGS.
        ..............

WRITE-FOOTERS.
        ..............
```

Example 9.11 Outline Procedure Division for report program

To run this program a customer file must first be set up on the system and populated with appropriate data.

10 Repeated Data Items

This chapter introduces arrays, arrays of record, and multi-dimensional arrays and shows how equivalent COBOL data structures may be created and accessed using subscripts. It also introduces the use of the REDEFINES clause for initialisation. The final section, which covers indexing and the SEARCH verb may be omitted on a first reading.

10.1 Introduction to Arrays

The concept of an array is fundamental to programming, and may be defined as a subscripted variable or alternatively, as a repeated data item. Each element of an array is of the same type. Elements of the array are mapped on to a sequence of memory locations, and individual elements may be identified and accessed by a subscript value.

In Pascal we might declare an array and subscript as in example 10.1

```
VAR     StudentMark : ARRAY[1..8] OF Integer;
        MarkIndex : 1..8;
```

Example 10.1 One-dimensional array and subscript in Pascal

A similar COBOL structure, usually referred to as a table, could be declared as in example 10.2

```
01 WS-STUDENT-REC.
   03 WS-STUDENT-MARK  PIC 99
        OCCURS 8 TIMES.
01  WS-MARK-INDEX    PIC 9.
```

Example 10.2 Repeated item and subscript in COBOL

A repeated data item may be an elementary or a group item, and is signified by an OCCURS clause as shown in example 10.2. The repeated item has been declared at level 3 since the OCCURS clause may not be used at level 1.

WS-STUDENT-REC is a group field that will hold 16 digits and so could be assigned a value such as

| 4 6 | 6 7 | 7 6 | 3 2 | 4 5 | 6 4 | 5 3 | 5 2 |

Any two-digit element could be accessed by referencing WS-STUDENT-MARK using a subscript. For example

```
DISPLAY  WS-STUDENT-MARK(5)
```

would print 45 on the screen, the value of the fifth occurrence.

We should note that parentheses are used for subscripting whereas Pascal uses square brackets. The subscript must be a positive numeric literal or a numeric data item.

Most implementations will not allow expressions as subscripts. Whereas in Pascal we could refer to StudentMark(MarkIndex+1), in COBOL it would be necessary to increment WS-MARK-INDEX before the subscription.

```
ADD 1 TO  MARK-INDEX.
DISPLAY  WS-MARK(WS-MARK-INDEX).
```

10.2 Arrays of Records

We sometimes need to store a sequence of records in main memory. As an example we may consider a data structure which is required to store a salesman number, the total sales made by the salesman for the period, and the total made for the previous period.

We could store the cumulative totals, the previous total and the related salesman numbers in three arrays

```
VAR SalesmanNo : ARRAY[1..50] OF Integer;
    SalesTotal  : ARRAY[1..50] OF Real;
    PreviousTotal : ARRAY[1..50] OF Real;
```

Example 10.3 Fields of a record in three Pascal arrays

with related items stored in the same position in each array as in example 10.3. If the number 1000 is in location 20 of the SalesmanNo array, then the values for SalesmanNo 1000's current and previous total sales will be in the same location of their respective arrays:

20 | 1000 | | 1987.65 | | 2543.45 |

SalesmanNo   SalesTotal   PreviousTotal

A similar COBOL table is shown in example 10.4.

```
01 SALES-TABLE.
   03 WS-SALESMAN-NO        PIC 9(4).
                OCCURS 50 TIMES.
   03 WS-SALES-TOTAL        PIC 9(4)V99
                OCCURS 50 TIMES.
   03 WS-PREVIOUS-TOTAL     PIC 9(4)V99
                OCCURS 50 TIMES.
```

Example 10.4 Fields of a record in three COBOL tables

The problem with the solution used in examples 10.3 and 10.4 is that each logical salesman-record cannot be accessed as a single entity, because each is distributed across three separate data structures. For languages which allow it, the correct solution is to use a single array, an array of record, so that the fields of a record can be stored contiguously.

	1000	(Salesman Number field)
20	1987.65	(Total Sales)
	2543.45	(Previous total)
	987	(Salesman Number field)
21	1567.00	(Total Sales)
	2000.18	(Previous total)

This could be realised in Pascal as in example 10.5.

```
TYPE   SalesmanRec = RECORD
              SalesmanNo : Integer;
              SalesTotal : Real;
              PreviousTotal : Real
         END;

VAR    Salesman : ARRAY[1..50] OF SalesmanRec;
```

Example 10.5 Pascal array of record

The 20th record would be accessed as

```
Salesman[20]
```

and the sales total contained in the 20th item would be accessed as

```
Salesman[20].SalesTotal
```

Learners sometimes find these structures difficult to master in Pascal, perhaps partly because of the notation required to access an individual field in an array of record. In COBOL the rules for accessing fields are less strict and perhaps more natural, and beginners seem to have fewer difficulties. A similar table in COBOL could be declared as follows:

```
01 SALES-TABLE.
    03 WS-SALESMAN-REC  OCCURS 50 TIMES.
        05 WS-SALESMAN-NO      PIC 9(4).
        05 WS-SALES-TOTAL      PIC 9(4)V99.
        05 WS-PREVIOUS-TOTAL   PIC 9(4)V99.
```

Example 10.6 COBOL repeated group item

The 20th occurrence of WS-SALESMAN-REC could be accessed as

```
WS-SALESMAN-REC(20)
```

The 20th occurrence of WS-SALES-TOTAL could be accessed as

```
WS-SALES-TOTAL(20).
```

The difference is that COBOL allows the subscript to be used either at group or lower level, whereas Pascal allows it at group level only.

10.3 Multi-dimensional Arrays

A multi-dimensional array is one which requires more than one subscript to identify an element. COBOL 74 allows for a maximum of three subscripts, which is sufficient for most applications; COBOL 85 allows seven subscripts.

As an example, using a two-dimensional array we could create a data structure which would allow us to hold the total monthly sales for each month of the year for each of 20 department stores.

```
VAR Sales : ARRAY[1..20,1..12] OF Real;
```

Example 10.7 Two-dimensional array

The two-dimensional array declared in example 10.7 would map the sales for store 1 on to the first 12 memory locations, those for store 2 on the next 12 locations, and so on. To access the sales of store 5 in June (month 6) we would refer to

```
Sales[5,6]
```

which indicates that we wish to access the 54th element in the array (if store 1 begins in relative location 1, store 5 begins in relative location 49, store 6 in 61 and so on).

A similar table in COBOL would be as shown in example 10.8.

```
01 WS-STORE-SALES.
   03 WS-STORE OCCURS 20 TIMES.
      05 WS-MONTHLY-SALE PIC 9(8)V99
         OCCURS 12 TIMES.
```

Example 10.8 Nested OCCURS clause

This notation may initially seem less straightforward than the Pascal declaration; it indicates that the record WS-STORE-SALES contains a single group field, WS-STORE, which is repeated 20 times, and that each WS-STORE contains one elementary field, WS-MONTHLY-SALE, which is repeated 12 times.

We may access the data stored by referring to the data item WS-STORE, which requires one subscript, or the data item WS-MONTHLY-SALE, which requires two subscripts. If we wish to access the sales of store 5 for June we would refer to

```
WS-MONTHLY-SALE(5,6)
```

We could directly access all the monthly sales for a given store by using a single subscript for the group field,

```
WS-STORE(5)
```

but it should be apparent that we cannot directly obtain the sales of all the stores for a given month. WS-MONTHLY-SALE(6), for example, would produce a compilation error, since it requires two subscripts. If we wished to declare a data structure which allowed direct access to all the sales totals for a single month, we would need to declare the table as in example 10.9. The sales of store 5 in June would now be

```
WS-STORE-SALE(6,5)
```

and the overall sales for June could be accessed as

```
WS-MONTH(6).
```

We now cannot directly obtain all the monthly sales for a chosen store; the sales return for store 5 for example would be stored in relative position 5, 25, 45 and so on; to access each one we would need two subscripts, one for the number of the month as well as one for the store number: (1,5), (2,5), (3,5) and so on.

```
01 WS-STORE-SALES.
   03 WS-MONTH
      OCCURS  12 TIMES.
      05 WS-STORE-SALE    PIC 9(8)V99
      OCCURS 20 TIMES.
```

Example 10.9 Nested OCCURS (cf. example 10.8)

Initial difficulty is sometimes experienced over subscripting items declared in multi-dimensional tables. The number of subscripts required by any data item may be calculated by counting the number of OCCURS to which it is subject. An item is subject to an OCCURS if an OCCURS is used in its declaration or if it is subordinate to a group field in which an OCCURS is used.

10.4   Use of PERFORM with Tables

The use of the PERFORM VARYING UNTIL was introduced in chapter 6. Its use in table handling will be covered only briefly in this chapter. If we have a two-dimensional table as in examples 10.7 and 10.8 the Pascal outline for processing each element would be as follows:

```
FOR each store DO
   FOR each month DO
      process each sales value
```

The indentation of the program structure matches the indentation of the COBOL data structure (see example 10.8). To convert the Pascal into COBOL 74 we would use two PERFORM statements with the VARYING options used to increment each subscript; this solution would require a hierarchy of three paragraphs. To convert into COBOL 85 we could use nested in-line PERFORMS which would give a solution closer to Pascal.

10.5   Initialising tables

We have already seen that, like a number of modern languages, although not Pascal, COBOL allows a programmer to initialise variables when they are declared, using a VALUE clause (chapter 1). We should note that this may be done in the Working-Storage Section only, and not in the File Section.

Repeated data items may also be initialised using the VALUE clause at group level, as in example 10.10. It should be noted, however, that the value assigned must be alphanumeric since all group fields are considered to be alphanumeric. ZEROS is a figurative constant which may be assigned to both numeric and alphanumeric data items. It would not be possible to initialise the table with VALUE 12 or VALUE 1, since these are numeric literals.

```
01 WS-EXAM-TABLE VALUE ZEROS.
   03 WS-EXAM-RESULTS  OCCURS 3 TIMES.
      05  WS-SUBJECT-1      PIC 99.
      05  WS-SUBJECT-2      PIC 99.
      05  WS-SUBJECT-3      PIC 99.
```

Example 10.10 Initialising table at group level

It should be noted that VALUE cannot be used in an entry using the OCCURS, nor in a field subordinate to an entry using an OCCURS. We could not, therefore, use it at level 03 or 05 in the above example.

To initialise each item with an individual value we could do the following:

```
01 WS-EXAM-TABLE VALUE   "223456524456423960".
   03 WS-EXAM-RESULTS  OCCURS 3 TIMES.
      05  WS-SUBJECT-1      PIC 99.
      05  WS-SUBJECT-2      PIC 99.
      05  WS-SUBJECT-3      PIC 99.
```

Example 10.11 Initialising table using non-numeric literal

The effect of the above VALUE clause is to assign to the table the string of digit characters which are mapped on to the individual items as indicated below.

2 2	3 4	5 6	5 2	4 4	5 6	4 2	3 9	6 0
1(1)	2(1)	3(1)	1(2)	2(2)	3(2)	1(3)	2(3)	3(3)

WS-SUBJECT-

WS-SUBJECT-1(3) for example is assigned the the value 42.

The assignment of value to a table at the group level is not usually considered to be a sensible solution, particularly for larger tables. The following solution, using a REDEFINES, is clearer, less error prone and easier to amend.

```
01 WS-EXAM-TABLE.
   03 WS-INITIAL-VALUES.
      05 FILLER    PIC 99 VALUE 22.
      05 FILLER    PIC 99 VALUE 34.
      05 FILLER    PIC 99 VALUE 56.
      05 FILLER    PIC 99 VALUE 52.
      05 FILLER    PIC 99 VALUE 44.
      05 FILLER    PIC 99 VALUE 56.
      05 FILLER    PIC 99 VALUE 42.
      05 FILLER    PIC 99 VALUE 39.
      05 FILLER    PIC 99 VALUE 60.
   03 WS-EXAMINATIONS REDEFINES WS-INITIAL-VALUES.
      05 WS-EXAMS  OCCURS 3 TIMES.
         07 WS-SUBJECT-1  PIC 99.
         07 WS-SUBJECT-2  PIC 99.
         07 WS-SUBJECT-3  PIC 99.
```

Example 10.12 Table initialisation using REDEFINES clause

WS-INITIAL-VALUES is used for initialisation only. WS-EXAMINATIONS is allocated the same storage area as WS-INITIAL-VALUES, and is simply a different view of that storage area. The subscripted items which may be used to access and alter individual elements of the table are WS-EXAMS, WS-SUBJECT-1, WS-SUBJECT-2 and WS-SUBJECT-3.

The REDEFINES clause may not be used in an item that also has an OCCURS clause, and it should have the same level number as the item that it is redefining.

There is no equivalent of the REDEFINES in Pascal; it is a facility which can prove very useful.

10.6   Indexing

COBOL provides indexing as an alternative to subscripting. The main advantage of an index as compared with a subscript is one of efficiency; an index holds a binary value which represents the byte displacement from the beginning of the table, whereas a subscript holds an occurrence of an item. An example of the declaration of an index facility is given in example 10.13. It should be noted that the index, MARK-INDEX, which is associated with the table, WS-STUDENT-MARK, has no picture string.

```
01 WS-STUDENT-REC.
   03 WS-STUDENT-MARK  PIC 99 OCCURS 8 TIMES
                       INDEXED BY MARK-INDEX.
```

Example 10.13 Declaration of an index

The following diagram shows how WS-STUDENT-MARK could be mapped on to 16 bytes of memory, and shows the equivalent byte displacement and occurrence value for each.

| 54 | 36 | 48 | 57 | 46 | 60 | 42 | 45 |

Byte displacement 0 2 4 6 8 10 12 14
Occurrence 1 2 3 4 5 6 7 8

The first item in the above table could be subscripted using 1, but the index value would be 0; the fourth item would be subscripted using 4, but the displacement would be 6.

```
01   WS-CASH-PAYMENT-TABLE.
     03 WS-PAYMENT-TRANSACTION
               OCCURS 20 TIMES
               INDEXED BY PAY-IND.
        05 WS-TRANS-NO     PIC 9(4).
        05 WS-NAME         PIC X(30).
        05 WS-AMOUNT       PIC 9999V99.
        05 WS-CUST-NO      PIC X(6).

01   WS-CUST-SEARCH-NO   PIC X(6).


PROCEDURE DIVISION.
     ...........
     SET PAY-IND  TO 1.
     SEARCH    WS-PAYMENT-TRANSACTION
       AT END  PERFORM  TRANSACTION-NOT-FOUND-PARA
     WHEN WS-CUST-NO(PAY-IND) = WS-CUST-SEARCH-NO
        PERFORM PROCESS-TRANSACTION-DETAILS.
     ..........
PROCESS-TRANSACTION-DETAILS.
     ..........
TRANSACTION-NOT-FOUND-PARA.
```

Example 10.14 Use of SEARCH

Aside from efficiency considerations, the advantage of indexing is that it allows use of the SEARCH verb. In example 10.14 the table is searched for an element that matches the condition specified after the WHEN; when a match is found the code specified after the condition is executed and the table search is terminated; if no match is found, the code specified after the AT END is executed.

The SET verb is used to initialise the index, PAY-IND, to the element at which the programmer wishes the search to begin. The conversion of occurrence to a displacement is hidden from the programmer.

A more efficient non-linear search is available (see example 10.15); if this is used, the table must be declared with a key, and the items in the table should be in key order. The programmer cannot in this case choose the starting point of the search.

```
      01   WS-CASH-PAYMENT-TABLE.
          03 WS-PAYMENT-TRANSACTION
                      OCCURS 20 TIMES
                      ASCENDING-KEY WS-CUST-NO
                      INDEXED BY PAY-IND
              05 WS-TRANS-NO   PIC 9(6).
              05 WS-NAME       PIC X(30).
              05 WS-AMOUNT     PIC 9999V99.
              05 WS-CUST-NO    PIC X(6).

      PROCEDURE DIVISION.
          ............
          SEARCH ALL WS-PAYMENT-TRANSACTION
          AT END  PERFORM  TRANSACTION-NOT-FOUND-PARA
          WHEN WS-CUST-NO(PAY-IND) = WS-CUST-SEARCH-NO
              PERFORM PROCESS-TRANSACTION-DETAILS.
          ............
      PROCESS-TRANSACTION-DETAILS.
          ............
      TRANSACTION-NOT-FOUND-PARA.
```

Example 10.15 Implementation of non-linear search

Study Guide

The emphasis of the chapter has been on short examples showing how arrays, arrays of records and two-dimensional arrays can be implemented. Ensure that you understand the difference between each, how each can be declared, and how nested OCCURS items are subscripted. Re-read and make notes on the use of OCCURS and REDEFINES.

Practical Exercises

1. The following table stores the monthly sales for each department in 20 stores and certain other data about the stores.

```
01 WS-STORE-SALES.
   03 WS-STORE          OCCURS  20 TIMES.
      05 WS-STORE-NAME            PIC X(20).
      05  WS-MANAGERIAL-STAFF    PIC X(20)
                  OCCURS 6 TIMES.
      05 WS-DEPARTMENT
                  OCCURS 5 TIMES.
         07 WS-MONTHLY-SALE    PIC 9(6)V99
                  OCCURS 12 TIMES.
```

Work out
i) The subscripts required to access the total sales for October in Store 5 Department 3.
ii) The subscripts required to access all the monthly Sales for the 1st Department in Store 6.
iii) What data items would be referenced by the following

```
STORE(5)
```

iv) How to access the name of the 18th Store.
2. A table is required to store the names and telephone numbers of five people. Produce a suitable COBOL declaration and initialisation using REDEFINES. Enter and compile this.
3. The processing of repeated data items requires a repeated statement, most usefully the PERFORM VARYING (see chapter 6). Design and code the Procedure Division of a program that would display the contents of the following table in a matrix on the screen, using a slash to separate items on each row.

```
01  WS-TABLE.
   03 WS-ROW OCCURS 5.
      05 WS-ITEM PIC 99
                  OCCURS 5.
```

Enter and compile the program. Note that in order to execute this the table will require initialisation, and two subscripts will be required.
4. Refer to the practical exercise in chapter 4. Set up a suitable table to store all the items required to produce an invoice, and then design and code and test each paragraph previously left as a template.

11   Indexed Files

This chapter introduces indexed files and shows how they may be declared and randomly accessed in a COBOL program using the READ, WRITE, REWRITE and DELETE verbs and the INVALID KEY clause. Sections 11.5, 11.6 and 11.7 provide coverage of sequential and dynamic access, and the use of alternate keys. The section on sequential processing introduces the START verb. On a first reading these last three sections may be omitted.

11.1   Introduction to Indexed Files

An indexed file is one in which an item may be uniquely identified and retrieved using a key field within the record. Whereas with a sequential file we normally begin processing with the first record, an indexed file allows fast access to any record whose key is specified. This is done through a hierarchy of indexes which the system maintains in order to keep track of each record on the file.

Indexed files are useful for on-line systems which need to provide users with random enquiry and update facilities. They are not supported in Pascal, and this deficiency is arguably Pascal's greatest weakness as an applications language.

Processing indexed files requires more resources than processing sequential files. It should also be noted that deleted records are still physically present after deletion, so that periodically an indexed file needs compacting to reduce the disk space required.

Consideration needs to be given to backup in systems using indexed files. Sequential files which allow different generations to be kept are more secure. Indexed files are also not appropriate for processing that involves a high hit rate.

11.2   Selecting an Indexed File

COBOL allows us to access an indexed file *randomly*, using the key field to identify a record; *sequentially*, starting at a specified key and processing each in turn; or *dynamically*, which allows both sequential and random access. We will begin by looking at the standard way in which an indexed file is defined for random access.

The coding required to select an indexed file is given in example 11.1.

```
ENVIRONMENT DIVISION.
INPUT-OUTPUT SECTION.
FILE-CONTROL.
      SELECT   CUST-FILE
      ASSIGN TO   implementor-name
      ORGANIZATION IS INDEXED
      ACCESS MODE IS RANDOM
      RECORD KEY IS CUST-NO
      FILE STATUS IS   CUST-STATUS.
```

Example 11.1 Selection of indexed file

When random access is specified, the records may be processed in any order according to the value placed in the key field before the operation is performed.

The Record Key clause specifies the primary key, which uniquely identifies each record and must be defined in the record description for the file. It is not possible to change the contents of a record's primary key once a record has been created, except by deleting and then writing the record.

The File-Status clause is optional; the item referred to must be a two-byte character field described in Working-Storage. Every time that the file is processed the system moves a status code to the specified item; this status code may be accessed and is useful for error handling. The manual should be checked for the list of code numbers used.

11.3   Indexed File Description

The file description is the same as for sequential files, but care must be taken in the record description to define the key field with the same name already declared in the File-Control paragraph.

```
DATA DIVISION.
FILE SECTION.
FD   CUST-FILE.
     01   CUSTOMER-REC.
          03   CUST-NO       PIC   X(6).
          03   CUST-NAME     PIC   X(20).
          03   AMOUNT-OWING  PIC   9999V99.
WORKING-STORAGE SECTION.
     01 CUST-STATUS    PIC   X(2).
```

Example 11.2 Indexed file definition and record description

11.4   Performing Operations on Indexed Files

The following operations are defined:

Write: transfer a new record to the file from the record area; if a record with the same key exists then an error is detected by the system;

Read: transfer a record from the file into the record area; if the record whose key is specified is not on the file then an error is detected;

Delete: logically remove a record from the file; if the record whose key is specified is not on the file then an error is detected.

Rewrite: amend an existing record by transferring a record from the record area to the file; if the record whose key is specified is not on the file then an error is detected.

To be able to use all of these we must open the file for Input–Output

```
OPEN    I-O   CUST-FILE.
```

The rules for closing indexed files are the same as for sequential files, and all files used, whatever their organisation, may be closed in a single statement.

```
CLOSE CUST-FILE   ...       ...
```

We may now briefly look at each of the verbs used to operate on records in the file. With each we must specify a statement to be executed when an invalid operation is attempted (eg attempting to read using a key that does not exist on the file). We may also, in the 85 standard, specify a statement to be executed when the operation is valid.

We may begin with an example (11.3) which attempts to read a record from the file previously described. The effect will be to transfer from the file a record whose key corresponds to the value contained in the key field in the file's record area. If no matching key can be found on the file the action defined in the INVALID KEY clause is executed.

```
MOVE "AB1234" TO CUST-NO.
READ CUST-FILE
    INVALID KEY
        DISPLAY "Not on file".
```

Example 11.3 Reading an indexed file

To create a new record, the record must be assembled either in the record area or in a suitable record defined in Working-Storage. If the latter is chosen then the WRITE FROM form of the verb is used, as in examples

11.4 and 11.5, which assume the description in Working-Storage of a record, WS-CUSTOMER-REC, with elementary items corresponding to those belonging to PERSON-REC.

```
MOVE "LF1096"  TO WS-CUST-NO.
MOVE "BLENKINSOP" TO WS-CUST-NAME.
MOVE ZEROS TO WS-AMOUNT-OWING.
WRITE CUSTOMER-REC FROM WS-CUSTOMER-REC
    INVALID KEY
        DISPLAY "Failed to write record".
```

Example 11.4 Writing to an indexed file

The WRITE statement in example 11.5 attempts a read if a write is unsuccessful, so that the existing record with the matching key may be displayed on screen; if the read fails then a message to that effect is displayed on the screen. It would of course at this point be more sensible to examine the contents of CUST-STATUS and take appropriate action.

```
MOVE "LF1096"  TO  WS-CUST-NO.
MOVE "BLENKINSOP" TO WS-CUST-NAME.
MOVE ZEROS TO WS-AMOUNT-OWING.
WRITE CUSTOMER-REC FROM WS-CUSTOMER-REC
    INVALID KEY
        DISPLAY "Failed to write record"
        DISPLAY  WS-CUSTOMER-REC
        READ CUST-FILE
          INVALID KEY
            DISPLAY "Failed to read record"
          NOT INVALID KEY
            DISPLAY "Record already exists:"
            DISPLAY CUSTOMER-REC
        END-READ
    END-WRITE
```

Example 11.5 Use of NOT INVALID KEY clause, COBOL 85

The reader should note that example 11.5 makes use of the statement terminators and the NOT INVALID KEY clause which are available in the 85 standard only. It is possible, with a little more difficulty, to achieve the same results using the 74 standard.

To amend an existing record we would normally do a READ, alter the record in main memory, and then REWRITE the record. The INVALID KEY clause on the REWRITE would be executed if an attempt was made to REWRITE a record whose key did not match any record on the file.

To delete a record we use DELETE; the INVALID KEY clause would be executed if the record we wished to delete could not be found; note that we would normally use READ first, to ensure that the record we were about to delete was the correct one!

Example 11.6 amends the record written in examples 11.4 and 11.5. Example 11.7 deletes the same record.

```
MOVE "LF1096" TO  WS-CUST-NO.
MOVE "BLENKINSOP" TO WS-CUST-NAME.
MOVE 100.25 TO WS-AMOUNT-OWING.
REWRITE CUSTOMER-REC FROM WS-CUSTOMER-REC
    INVALID KEY
        DISPLAY "Record does not exist".
```

Example 11.6 Amending a record

It should be noted that whereas we WRITE and REWRITE a record (CUSTOMER-REC), we READ and DELETE a file (CUST-FILE). This is more logical than it seems. In a READ and a DELETE the system needs the key value only to identify the record required; the WRITE and REWRITE operations require the record name to be able to handle differing types and sizes of record on the same file.

```
MOVE "LF1096" TO  CUST-NO.
DELETE CUST-FILE
    INVALID KEY
    DISPLAY "Record does not exist".
```

Example 11.7 Deleting a record

11.5   Sequential Access

Indexed files may be processed sequentially starting either at the beginning or at a specified record. To process CUST-FILE sequentially we need to make only a single change to the entries in examples 11.1 and 11.2:

```
ACCESS IS RANDOM
```

now becomes

```
ACCESS IS SEQUENTIAL.
```

If we wished to read an indexed file sequentially we would open it for input

```
OPEN INPUT CUST-FILE
```

and we would read each record in turn using the READ ... AT END as in reading sequentially organised files. Records would be transferred in key sequence, beginning with the record with the lowest key.

If we wish to begin reading the file sequentially at a record other than the first we may use the START verb, which positions the file pointer on the required record, if that record exists (see example 11.8). We may then read the file sequentially using the READ .... AT END. It should be noted that the START does not transfer the record into the record area.

```
MOVE "MA0000" TO  CUST-NO.
START CUST-FILE
   INVALID KEY
      DISPLAY "Record does not exist".
```

Example 11.8 Use of START verb

An alternative form of the START statement allows a relation to be specified, as is shown in example 11.9.

```
MOVE "MA0000" TO  CUST-NO.
START CUST-FILE  KEY > CUST-NO
   INVALID KEY
      DISPLAY "No key greater than MA0000"
      MOVE "MB0000" TO CUST-NO.
IF CUST-NO NOT = "MB0000"
   READ CUST-FILE
      AT END
          MOVE "MB0000" TO CUST-NO.
PERFORM PROCESS-FILE UNTIL CUST-NO > "MA9999".
. . . . . . . . . . . .

PROCESS-FILE.
   . . . . . . . . . . . . . . . .
   READ CUST-FILE
   AT END
      MOVE "MB0000" TO CUST-NO.
```

Example 11.9 Use of START verb with KEY phrase

Example 11.9 shows how a sequence of records with keys in the range MA0001 to MA9999 would be read from an indexed file in key order. The key specified in the KEY phrase (CUST-NO in example 11.9) may be an alternate key (see section 11.7). If so, that key is used for subsequent sequential processing.

One difficulty that must be guarded against is the failure of the START to execute successfully, in which case the key and the file pointer are undefined. In example 11.9 this is dealt with in the INVALID KEY clause by moving a value outside the range required to the key. The same value is moved to the key if the end-of-file is encountered; this allows a single condition to be used to control the iteration. It should be noted that if the START fails, the PERFORM UNTIL will execute zero times.

It should be noted that the 85 standard provides for an optional NOT INVALID KEY clause and an END-START, both of which can greatly simplify the use of the START verb, as may be seen in example 11.10.

```
MOVE "MA0000" TO CUST-NO.
START CUST-FILE KEY > CUST-NO
    INVALID KEY
        DISPLAY "No key greater than MA0000"
        MOVE "MB0000" TO CUST-NO.

    NOT INVALID KEY
        READ CUST-FILE
        AT END
            MOVE "MB0000" TO CUST-NO

        END-READ
END-START
PERFORM UNTIL CUST-NO > "MA9999"
    ................
    READ CUST-FILE
    AT END
        MOVE "MB0000" TO CUST-NO
    END-READ
END-PERFORM
```

Example 11.10 START verb with NOT INVALID KEY phrase and statement terminators in COBOL 85

In example 11.10 it may be noted that the NOT INVALID KEY clause is used to read the first record. The END-START delimiter is deliberately placed before the PERFORM statement, since logically the reading and processing of a sequence of records should not be part of a START statement.

If we wish to create a new indexed file, normally using a sequential file as input, we must open the indexed file for sequential output:

```
OPEN OUTPUT CUST-FILE
```

and then use the WRITE verb with the INVALID KEY clause. A key is invalid if it is smaller than the last key written to the file. This ensures that an indexed file is created in key order. There is no restriction on the value of the first key on the file.

Finally, it should be noted that an indexed file with sequential access may be opened for I-O, in which case sequential updating in place may be carried out using the REWRITE and DELETE verbs; in each case the record processed is the last one read.

11.6 Dynamic Access

If dynamic access is specified in the File-Control paragraph then the programmer may change between using sequential and random access. If files are in this mode the READ ...... NEXT RECORD AT END must be used to indicate to the system that sequential reading is to take place.

```
        MOVE "MA0000" TO  CUST-NO.
        READ CUST-FILE
            INVALID KEY
                MOVE "F" TO WS-RECORD-FOUND.

    * This assumes a  data item  WS-RECORD-FOUND
    * with a level 88 condition-name, RECORD-FOUND VALUE "T".
    * WS-RECORD-FOUND is assumed to be set to "T" before the READ

        IF RECORD-FOUND
            READ CUST-FILE NEXT RECORD
            AT END
                MOVE "N" TO WS-RECORD-FOUND.
```

Example 11.11 Random and sequential READ : dynamic access

In example 11.11 the program would attempt a random read of the record with key MA0000, and then if successful would read the next record in key order. Note that this would not necessarily be MA0001, and if MA0000 were the last record on file then the AT END phrase would be executed.

11.7   Alternate Keys

It is possible to declare secondary keys for an indexed file. Each alternate key must be an alphanumeric item in a record declared in the file description entry. Alternate keys are specified in the File-Control paragraph as shown in example 11.12.

```
ENVIRONMENT DIVISION.
INPUT-OUTPUT SECTION.
FILE-CONTROL.
      SELECT   CUST-FILE
      ASSIGN TO implementor-name
      ORGANIZATION IS INDEXED
      ACCESS MODE IS DYNAMIC
      RECORD KEY IS CUST-NO
      ALTERNATE RECORD KEY IS CUST-NAME
      FILE STATUS IS   CUST-STATUS.
```

Example 11.12 Indexed file with alternate key

Alternate keys should be unique unless the programmer specifies otherwise by the addition of the DUPLICATES phrase:

ALTERNATE RECORD KEY IS CUST-NAME **WITH DUPLICATES**

An alternate key may be specified in READ statements and START statements. The programmer might for example wish to retrieve all the JONES entries on the customer file, and this could be coded as shown in example 11.13.

```
MOVE "JONES"  TO  CUST-NAME.
READ CUST-FILE
   KEY IS CUST-NAME
   INVALID KEY
        MOVE ALL "Z" TO CUST-NAME.
PERFORM READ-AND-DISPLAY
        UNTIL CUST-NAME > "JONES".
   . . . . . . . . . . . .
READ-AND-DISPLAY.
   DISPLAY CUSTOMER-REC.
   READ CUST-FILE NEXT RECORD
      AT END
        MOVE ALL "Z" TO CUST-NAME.
```

Example 11.13 Alternate key in READ statement: dynamic access

It should be noted that the successful execution of the first read establishes CUST-NAME as the key being used for CUST-FILE until it is altered by another KEY phrase. The KEY phrase may not be used with an AT END phrase.

Study Suggestions

This chapter has covered indexed files. You are recommended to make notes on the Environment and Data Division entries required, and to check your manual for implementation dependent features.

You are also advised to make notes on random access, noting how an indexed file must be opened, and how each operation is used in that access mode.

You should also make notes on the use of the INVALID KEY clause, and the conditions under which it is executed, and on the use of the FILE-STATUS word, and of the START verb.

Practical Exercises

1. Check the installation manual as to how an indexed file may be set up, and set up the file specified in examples 11.1 and 11.2. Implement a program which allows a user to interrogate this file interactively. The top level design for this program may be specified as follows

```
Open CustomerFile
Read UserSelection from keyboard
WHILE NOT Quit DO
BEGIN
  CASE SELECTION OF
   'A' : AmendRecord;
   'C' : CreateRecord;
   'D' : DeleteRecord;
   'R' : RetrieveRecord;
   'Q' :
  END
END;
Close File
```

AmendRecord, CreateRecord, DeleteRecord and RetrieveRecord may be implemented as separate paragraphs called from a PERFORM statement. The While and the Case should be implemented using the appropriate constructs depending on whether COBOL 85 or COBOL 74 is being used (see chapter 5).

2. Add an option which allows a user to specify a range of records to be displayed; note that this will require Dynamic Access.

12 Relative Files

This chapter introduces relative files and provides a brief guide only to their use. Relative files are not as widely used as sequential and indexed files, and this chapter may well be omitted on a first reading.

12.1 Introduction to Relative Files

A relative file is a file whose records are uniquely identified by a relative integer greater than zero. Relative files provide faster access than indexed files because the key used to identify a record determines the physical position of the record on the file. If, for example, we declare a file in which the data for each record is 20 bytes long, the record whose key = 5 will begin in the 81st byte. Some implementations of Pascal allow such files to be created and accessed, but none is likely to provide the high-level facilities available in COBOL, which are very similar to those described in chapter 11 for indexed files.

Relative files are ideally suited to cases in which records are self-indexing. One such example would be a file containing a periodic table of elements in which details about each element were stored in a position determined by its element number - for example hydrogen would be stored in relative position 1, helium in position 2, and so on. This is unfortunately an atypical application: the file is non-volatile, each record is uniquely identified by a key field, and there are no gaps in the sequence. For most applications it is difficult to find an algorithm that allows a unique relative number to be generated from one or more fields of a record without leaving a lot of empty space in the file. This difficulty explains why indexed files, despite slower access, are more widely used than relative files.

12.2 Relative File Selection and Description

The coding required to select a relative file is given in example 12.1.

```
ENVIRONMENT DIVISION.
INPUT-OUTPUT SECTION.
```

```
FILE-CONTROL.
        SELECT  PERSONNEL-FILE
        ASSIGN TO   implementor-name
        ORGANIZATION IS RELATIVE
        ACCESS MODE IS RANDOM
        RELATIVE KEY IS PERSON-NO
        FILE STATUS IS  PFILE-STATUS.
```

Example 12.1 Selection of a relative file

It should be noted that the only alterations from an indexed file are
1.The ORGANIZATION clause specifies RELATIVE;
2.The RELATIVE KEY must be specified as shown in example 12.1; the
RELATIVE KEY must be an unsigned numeric item; it must *not* be
declared as part of the file's associated record description and should
normally be declared in the Working-Storage Section.

```
DATA DIVISION.
FILE SECTION.
FD   PERSONNEL-FILE.
     01  PERSON-REC.
         03 NAT-INS-NUMBER          PIC XX999999X.
         03 DATE-JOINED             PIC  X(6).
         03 EMPLOYEE-NAME           PIC  X(20).
         03 SALARY                  PIC  9(5).

WORKING-STORAGE SECTION.
     01 PFILE-STATUS    PIC  X(2).
     01 PERSON-NO       PIC  9(4).
```

Example 12.2 Relative file definition and record description

In example 12.1 the record key is the data item PERSON-NO which is
declared in the Working-Storage Section as a PIC 9(4) field (example
12.2). The data item PFILE-STATUS is a two-byte item which may be
inspected after an operation has been performed (see section 11.2).

12.3   Processing a Relative File: Random Access

The file should be opened as for indexed files

```
OPEN    I-O   PERSONNEL-FILE.
```

To transfer a record from the file we first move a value to the data item defined as the RELATIVE KEY. We then attempt a READ with an INVALID KEY phrase; the statement following INVALID KEY will execute if the matching key cannot be found on the file. Example 12.3 shows how record number 1008 would be read from the file.

```
MOVE 1008 TO PERSON-NO.
READ PERSONNEL-FILE
    INVALID KEY
        DISPLAY "Key " PERSON-NO " Not on file".
```

Example 12.3 Reading a record from a relative file

If the record was not present the message

```
"Key 1008 Not on file"
```

would be displayed.

The reader should now be able to work out how records could be deleted, written and rewritten. If necessary you are advised to look back to chapter 11 to see how these verbs are used for indexed files.

12.4   Sequential Access

The rules for processing a relative file sequentially are similar to those for indexed files:
1. SEQUENTIAL rather than RANDOM should be specified in the access clause;
2. The file is opened for INPUT or OUTPUT.

The WRITE statement needs added comment, however. When a relative file is written sequentially, the first record written to the file is given the relative number one, and the number of each subsequent record is incremented automatically.

The START verb may be used with relative files, and always references the relative key. Example 12.4 shows how a record with a relative key greater than 100 would be defined as the starting point for sequential processing. If present, the first such record would be retrieved

```
MOVE 100 TO PERSON-NO.
START PERSONNEL-FILE KEY > PERSON-NO
    INVALID KEY
        DISPLAY "No record  number > " PERSON-NO
                        " on file".
```

Example 12.4 Use of START verb with relative file

by the next read (refer to section 11.5 for comparison with indexed files); if not present the statement following the INVALID KEY phrase would be executed.

12.5   Dynamic Access

The rules for dynamic access are similar to those for indexed files; they allow the programmer to change between using sequential and random access.

```
MOVE 1000  TO  PERSON-NO
READ PERSONNEL-FILE
   INVALID KEY
         DISPLAY "No record number > " PERSON-NO " on file".
         MOVE 9999 TO PERSON-NO.
PERFORM READ-AND-DISPLAY
         UNTIL PERSON-NO > 1999

      ............
READ-AND-DISPLAY.
   DISPLAY PERSON-REC.
   READ PERSONNEL-FILE NEXT RECORD
         AT END
         MOVE 9999 TO PERSON-NO.
```

Example 12.5 Relative file: dynamic access

Example 12.5 would display on the screen all records on the file with numbers in the sequence 1000 to 1999, provided that a record with Person-No 1000 existed. When the end-of-file is encountered the value 9999 is moved to the key field; this automatically terminates the loop.

Study Suggestions

This chapter has provided a very brief introduction to the use of relative files; the reader is advised to make notes on the Environment Division entries required, and to note the way in which the relative key is specified and declared; the reader is also advised to check the installation manual for implementation dependent rules governing the use of relative files.

Practical Exercises

1. Find out from your manual how to create a relative file, and create a file that will store records such as those defined in examples 12.1 and 12.2. Write a program that allows a user to interrogate this file interactively. (For the detailed design of a similar program see the practical exercise in chapter 11.)

2. Add an option which requests a user to enter a start and end-key, and then prints out the names that fall within the range specified. (Note, this will require dynamic access).

Part 4

Modular Structures

13   Separately Compiled Subprograms

This chapter discusses concepts of modularity, data abstraction and data hiding, and introduces the facilities provided in COBOL for the separate compilation and calling of subprograms. The material in this and the next chapter goes beyond the requirements of a first course in COBOL.

13.1   Modularity

When large software systems are being produced, particularly those involving more than one programmer working in parallel, it is essential to be able to break a system down into separate modules. Each module may then be designed, coded and tested independently using a driver program, before the system is linked and tested. A well-designed modular system should allow changes to be localised, and therefore make software maintenance easier. It should also, in theory at least, enable installations to build libraries of reliable, reusable modules.

Current academic ideas on modularity emphasise the importance of identifying data structures as well as functions when breaking a system down into modules. Recent languages such as Modula-2 and Ada, which have been derived from Pascal, allow each data structure and its associated procedures to be encapsulated within an independent program unit. They also support principles of data abstraction and data hiding by separating a module interface or system-builder view from an implementation or programmer view. A programmer view involves how a module is coded on a particular machine, whereas a system builder works at a higher level of abstraction and is concerned solely with what a module does and how it is used within the system being constructed.

We can illustrate these ideas with an example. We can begin with an informal specification of a module, which we can call Stock-Module.
Stock-Module.
This will consist of a list of products. The list will consist of 1000-1200 items. Each item in the list consists of

121

code number
price
description
quantity-in-stock.

Operations to be performed on the list are

Add a product to list
Remove a product from list
Return the complete entry for a product
Alter the price for a product
Alter the quantity-in-stock for a product

We may further define each operation informally

Add a product to list
User supplies code, description, price, quantity-in-stock;
If the code is not unique the operation is unsuccessful and an error message is passed back;
If the operation is successful a 'Done' message is passed back.

Remove a product from list
User supplies code;
If the code does not exist the operation is unsuccessful and an error message is passed back;
If the operation is successful a 'Done' message is passed back.

Return the complete entry for a product
User supplies code;
If the code does not exist the operation is unsuccessful and an error message is passed back;
If the operation is successful a 'Done' message is passed back and a complete item record also passed back.

Alter the price for a product
User supplies code and new price;
If the code does not exist the operation is unsuccessful and an error message is passed back;
If the code exists the existing price is replaced by the new price and a 'Done' message is passed back.

Alter the quantity-in-stock for a product
User supplies code, and amount to add or subtract;
If the code does not exist the operation is unsuccessful and an error message is passed back;
If the amount to be subtracted is greater than the existing quantity-in-stock an error message is passed back;
If the code exists the quantity in stock is altered and a 'Done' message is passed back.

From this specification, an interface to the module may be written and agreed by the programmer and the system builder; the module will provide each of the operations defined. The programmer may then construct the module required. Users of the module need to know only how to use each operation, and need know nothing about how the data structure is implemented. It could be a relative file or an indexed file, or even a sequential file read into a table in main memory. We may say then that the data structure is hidden from the user, who has only an abstract view of it; equally importantly, the data structure is protected from misuse by the user, who can access it only through the defined operations.

Building software in this way requires facilities for separate compilation. Pascal was designed as a small, compact language for teaching programming principles rather than as a tool for constructing large systems, and does not support standard separate compilation facilities. COBOL, however, does provide standard facilities for communication between separately compiled programs linked into a single run unit.

We shall, later in the chapter, show in outline how COBOL would allow us to develop and call the module specified. First, we need to clarify the difference between a subprogram and a Pascal subroutine.

13.2   Procedures, Functions and Subprograms

Readers will presumably be familiar with the use of procedures and functions as implemented in Pascal. Each procedure and function may have access to local data declared in its own block, as well as access to global data declared in surrounding blocks. Pascal also provides for the use of parameters which allow values to be passed in and out of procedures.

The crucial distinction between a subprogram as implemented in COBOL and a procedure or function in Pascal is that while the latter have inputs and outputs, a subprogram also has a state. We may illustrate this with example 13.1, in Pascal which has inputs only. Procedure Addint would at each entry create a new array, and would store the value passed in as X in the Kth position. On exit the whole array would be lost. During execution of the procedure the array ListOfIntegers would never contain more than a single integer, and each location other than the Kth location would be undefined.

```
PROCEDURE AddInt (K,X Integer);
VAR ListOfIntegers : ARRAY[1..100] OF Integer;
BEGIN
    ListOfIntegers[K] := X
END; (*Addint*)
```

Example 13.1 Pascal procedure with parameters and local variable

The solution to this problem would be to declare ListOfIntegers as a global variable, but this removes the protection which encapsulation of the array in a procedure brings.

A COBOL subprogram could be defined for this as in example 13.2. It should be noted that this allows repeated access to the table of integers from the time the subprogram is first called until the end of the program, and at the same time it protects the table from being accessed by another subprogram.

```
        IDENTIFICATION DIVISION.
        PROGRAM-ID. LIST.


        ENVIRONMENT DIVISION.


        DATA DIVISION.
        WORKING-STORAGE SECTION.
          01  LIST-OF-INTEGERS VALUE ZERO.
              03 WS-ITEM OCCURS 100   PIC X(9).


        LINKAGE SECTION.
          01  LOCATION             PIC 999.
          01  IN-VALUE             PIC 9(9).


        PROCEDURE DIVISION USING LOCATION IN-VALUE.
        MAIN-PARA.
            MOVE IN-VALUE TO WS-ITEM(LOCATION).
        END-PARA.
            EXIT PROGRAM.
```

Example 13.2 A COBOL subprogram

If the subprogram was called with the following successive pairs of values passed in as parameters

```
            15     20
            100    500
            18     96
```

then its successive states would be as follows:

Location	Entry 1	Exit 1	Entry 2	Exit 2	Entry 3	Exit 3
15	0	20	20	20	20	20
100	0	0	0	5000	5000	5000
18	0	0	0	0	0	96

Each data item would be set to the initial value specified in the VALUE clause on the first call only. Unlike a Pascal procedure or function, therefore, the program would maintain its state between calls, so that, for example, the state on entry the 3rd time is the same as the state on exit the 2nd time.

It would be possible, by defining an additional parameter in the Linkage Section, to allow the subprogram to carry out more than one operation as shown in the program in example 13.3, which retrieves as well as stores values.

```
IDENTIFICATION DIVISION.
PROGRAM-ID. LIST.

ENVIRONMENT DIVISION.

DATA DIVISION.
WORKING-STORAGE SECTION.
    01  LIST-OF-INTEGERS VALUE ZERO.
        03 WS-ITEM OCCURS 100   PIC X(9).

LINKAGE SECTION.
    01  LOCATION            PIC 999.
    01  IN-OUT-VALUE        PIC 9(9).
    01 OPERATION-CODE       PIC X.
        88   ADD-INT VALUE "A".
        88   RETRIEVE-INT VALUE "R".
PROCEDURE DIVISION USING    LOCATION
                            OPERATION-CODE
                            IN-OUT-VALUE.
MAIN-PARA.
    IF ADD-INT
        MOVE IN-OUT-VALUE TO WS-ITEM(LOCATION)
    ELSE IF RETRIEVE-INT
            MOVE WS-ITEM(LOCATION) TO IN-OUT-VALUE.
* If retrieve is required the value in the required location
* is placed in IN-OUT-VALUE.
    END-PARA.
        EXIT PROGRAM.
```

Example 13.3 Storage and retrieval in a table in a subprogram

It should be straightforward to work out how other operations could be added to the subprogram to allow search and removal of integers to take place.

13.3   Separate Compilation Facilities in COBOL

As may be seen in example 13.3, a COBOL subprogram differs only in minor respects from the COBOL programs previously covered. The differences may be summarised as follows:

i) If parameters are to be used then these should be defined in a Linkage Section in the Data Division; parameters are declared in the same way as data items previously used.

ii) The parameters to be used should be appended to the Procedure Division header in a USING phrase as shown in example 13.3.

iii) The subprogram should have one or more EXIT PROGRAM statements to return control to the calling program. Each EXIT PROGRAM statement must be the only statement in a paragraph. In example 13.3 it is in END-PARA.

A program which can call the subprogram defined in example 13.3, is shown in example 13.4. The CALL statement shown in the example passes the values 23 "A" and 2345 to the called program. This would be interpreted by the called program defined in example 13.3 as a request to store the value 2345 in location 23. It should be noted that the string of characters "LIST" is the program name of the called program, *not* the name of the file in which the source or object program is stored.

```
IDENTIFICATION DIVISION.
PROGRAM-ID. MAIN.

ENVIRONMENT DIVISION.

DATA DIVISION.
WORKING-STORAGE SECTION.
    01   WS-LOCATION          PIC 999.
    01   WS-VALUE             PIC 9(9).
    01   WS-OP-CODE           PIC X.

PROCEDURE DIVISION.
MAIN-PARA.
        . . . . . . . . . . . . .
    MOVE 23 TO WS-LOCATION.
    MOVE "A" TO WS-OP-CODE.
    MOVE  2345 TO WS-VALUE.
    CALL "LIST" USING WS-LOCATION
                      WS-OP-CODE
                      WS-VALUE.
        . . . . . . . . . . . . . .
```

Example 13.4 Calling a COBOL subprogram

It should be noted that the order of the parameters in the USING phrase should be the same in the calling as in the called program since the actual parameters will be matched by position at run time. The data items used to pass parameters from the calling program should be the same size as those in the called program. Data names only may be used as actual parameters. It is not permissible to use parameters such as "A", 25 or 12*2.

Pascal allows for two different types of parameter, value parameters and variable parameters. When value parameters are used, values are passed into the called subroutine and nothing is returned. When variable parameters are used, values may be passed in and out of the procedure. In Pascal, variable parameters are distinguished from value parameters by placing the reserved word VAR before the parameter in the procedure or function heading:

```
PROCEDURE FindGreater (VAR Greater: Integer, X,Y; Integer);
```

In the above example the parameter Greater is a variable parameter and would be used to pass out the greater of the values passed in via X and Y which are value parameters. This is implemented by passing an address to the procedure, and any alteration made to the parameter is immediately made to the location referenced by the address passed.

COBOL 74 supports variable parameters only, and the default in COBOL 85 is for variable parameters. But, in addition, COBOL 85 allows the programmer of a calling program to specify whether parameters are to be value parameters (BY CONTENT in COBOL) or variable parameters (BY REFERENCE in COBOL). This important difference from Pascal should be noted. COBOL 85 leaves the decision to be made by the user of the subprogram rather than the supplier of the subprogram; this means of course that the same parameter may be substituted at different times BY REFERENCE and BY CONTENT.

In example 13.4, which could be used in both COBOL 74 and 85, each parameter is passed by reference. In example 13.5, which is allowed in COBOL 85 only, two parameters are defined as being passed BY CONTENT (a value parameter in Pascal) and the third, which is required to receive a value from the subprogram, is passed BY REFERENCE (a variable parameter in Pascal).

The effect of the call in example 13.5, would be to request the subprogram to retrieve the value from location 23. The calling program would be protected from any alteration made to the parameters passed BY CONTENT, but the contents of location 23 would be passed back using WS-VALUE, which is passed BY REFERENCE.

```
         IDENTIFICATION DIVISION.
         PROGRAM-ID. MAIN.

         ENVIRONMENT DIVISION.

         DATA DIVISION.
         WORKING-STORAGE SECTION.
             01  WS-LOCATION          PIC XX.
             01  WS-VALUE             PIC X(9).
             01  WS-OP-CODE           PIC X.


         PROCEDURE DIVISION.
         MAIN-PARA.
             . . . . . . . . . . . . . .
             MOVE 23 TO WS-LOCATION.
             MOVE "R" TO WS-OP-CODE.
             CALL "LIST" USING  BY CONTENT WS-LOCATION
                                           WS-OP-CODE
                                BY REFERENCE WS-VALUE.

             . . . . . . . . . . . . . .
```

Example 13.5 Passing parameters BY CONTENT and BY REFERENCE,
COBOL 85 only

13.4 Restoring a Called Program to its Initial State

It has been explained previously that a COBOL subprogram maintains its
state when it exits. A facility is available to restore the subprogram to its
initial state. This may be done by using the CANCEL verb. The statement

```
    CANCEL "LIST"
```

will achieve this. It must be positioned in the calling program, and should
be executed after a called program has exited. When a subprogram is
cancelled the memory required is released, which may be necessary if a run
unit is operating within tight memory constraints.

COBOL 85 provides an alternative way of restoring a subprogram to its
initial state. Any COBOL program may be declared an 'Initial' program as
shown in example 13.6. The use of the INITIAL phrase ensures that on
each call it will, like a Pascal procedure, automatically be restored to its
initial state.

```
IDENTIFICATION DIVISION.
PROGRAM-ID. LIST IS INITIAL.

..............
```
Example 13.6 Use of INITIAL phrase, COBOL 85

13.5 Extended Example of Data Hiding Using Separate Compilation Facilities

We may now see how the example introduced in the first section of the chapter may be implemented in COBOL. Our data structure may be encapsulated in a separate module or program, STOCKMODULE, and we will in this instance implement it using an indexed file. On first entry the subprogram opens the file and moves "O" to a status variable, WS-MODULE-STATUS.

```
IDENTIFICATION DIVISION.
PROGRAM-ID. STOCKMODULE.
ENVIRONMENT DIVISION.
INPUT-OUTPUT SECTION.
FILE-CONTROL.
     SELECT   STOCK-FILE
     ASSIGN TO   implementor-name
     ORGANIZATION IS INDEXED
     ACCESS MODE IS RANDOM
     RECORD KEY IS ITEM-NO
     FILE STATUS IS   STOCK-FILE-STATUS.

DATA DIVISION.
FILE SECTION.
FD   STOCK-FILE.
     01  STOCK-REC.
         03  ITEM-NO                PIC  X(6).
         03  ITEM-DESCRIPTION       PIC  X(20).
         03  ITEM-PRICE             PIC  9999V99.
         03  QUANTITY-IN-STOCK      PIC  9(8).

WORKING-STORAGE SECTION.
     01 STOCK-FILE-STATUS        PIC  X(2).
     01 WS-MODULE-STATUS         PIC  X
              VALUE "I".
         88 INITIAL-STATE      VALUE "I".
```

```
LINKAGE SECTION.
01   ITEM                        PIC X(6).
01   DESC                        PIC X(20).
01   PRICE                       PIC  9999V99.
01   QTY                         PIC 9(8).
01   OPERATION-CODE              PIC X.
     88   ADD-ITEM          VALUE "A".
     88   RETRIEVE-ITEM     VALUE "R".
     88   ALTER-PRICE       VALUE "P".
     88   DELETE-ITEM       VALUE "D".
     88   ALTER-QUANTITY    VALUE "Q".
     88   CLOSE-DOWN        VALUE "C".
01   OPERATION-STATUS            PIC X.
     88   FAILED-OPERATION
                  VALUE "F".
     88   OPERATION-DONE
                  VALUE "D".


PROCEDURE DIVISION USING ITEM DESC PRICE QTY
                    OPERATION-CODE   OPERATION-STATUS.
MAIN-PARA.
     IF INITIAL-STATE
        OPEN I-O STOCK-FILE
        MOVE "O" TO WS-MODULE-STATUS.
     MOVE "D" TO OPERATION-STATUS.
* Assume initially that operation is successful
* Lower-level paragraphs will alter this if the operation fails
     IF ADD-ITEM
        PERFORM ADD-ITEM-PARA
     ELSE IF RETRIEVE-ITEM
             PERFORM RETRIEVE-ITEM-PARA
     ELSE IF DELETE-ITEM
             PERFORM DELETE-ITEM-PARA
     ELSE IF ALTER-PRICE
             PERFORM ALTER-PRICE-PARA
     ELSE IF ALTER-QUANTITY
             PERFORM ALTER-QUANTITY-PARA
     ELSE IF CLOSE-DOWN
             PERFORM CLOSE-DOWN-PARA
     ELSE MOVE "F" TO OPERATION-STATUS.


EXIT-PARA.
     EXIT PROGRAM.
```

```
ADD-ITEM-PARA.
    MOVE ITEM TO ITEM-NO.
    MOVE DESC TO DESCRIPTION.
    MOVE PRICE TO ITEM-PRICE.
    MOVE QTY TO QUANTITY-IN-STOCK.
    WRITE STOCK-REC
        INVALID KEY MOVE "F" TO OPERATION-STATUS.


DELETE-ITEM-PARA.
* This and succeeding paragraphs are templates only.


RETRIEVE-ITEM-PARA.


ALTER-PRICE-PARA.


ALTER-QUANTITY-PARA.


CLOSE-DOWN-PARA.
```

Example 13.7 Called program encapsulating indexed file

We have in example 13.7 created a module which consists of a data structure and six operations that may be used to access the structure. This technique protects the data structure by carefully controlling access and provides an abstract view of the operations that may be performed on the data structure; this simplifies the tasks of others involved in using and maintaining the software. The resulting module, although requiring more code than if embedded in the main program, is totally independent, and likely to be easy to maintain and to reuse in a number of applications. Since even relatively simple COBOL programs require a comparatively large number of lines of code, there are additional advantages in splitting what would otherwise be unmanageably large source programs into modules.

Finally, the reader is recommended to look at the implementation manual for guidance as to the compilation and linking of a run unit containing one or more subprograms. As a general rule it is necessary to compile each subprogram and the main program, and then to link the main program, each compiled program, and the COBOL library into an executable run unit.

Study Guide

This chapter has covered separate compilation, including the use of parameters, the Linkage Section, and the use of the CALL verb with parameters. It has also covered the COBOL 85 facility that allows parameters to be passed BY CONTENT and BY REFERENCE. It is recommended that notes are made on the Linkage Section, the CALL verb, BY CONTENT and BY REFERENCE, and that the distinction between a procedure as implemented in Pascal and a subprogram as implemented in COBOL is noted. Note should also be taken of the IS INITIAL phrase (COBOL 85 only) and the CANCEL verb.

Practical Exercises

1. Code a subprogram which receives a string of characters as a parameter, displays the characters on the screen, accepts a numeric item from the keyboard, and passes it back using another parameter to the calling program. For example the message could be 'enter a number >'. Compile and execute this subprogram using a suitable calling program.

2. Complete the coding of STOCKMODULE begun in example 13.7, compile and execute this program using a suitable calling program. (The design suggested for the exercise in chapter 11 could with modification be used here, using parameterised calls to the subprogram instead of performing paragraphs.)

14 Nested Subprograms

This chapter introduces facilities available in COBOL 85 which allow programs to be nested, and allow the declaration of global as well as local data.

14.1 Nested Programs

COBOL 85 allows programs to be nested. To do this the nested programs must be entered after the Procedure Division of the main program, and an End-program header must be placed after the nested programs. An End-program header for a program called MAIN would consist of

```
END PROGRAM MAIN.
```

It should be noted that, rather confusingly, there is no hyphen between END and PROGRAM.

If we wished to nest two programs, PROGA1 and PROGA2 within program MAIN they would be entered as shown in outline below.

```
*                                  MAIN____
      IDENTIFICATION DIVISION.
      PROGRAM-ID. MAIN.
      ...............
      PROCEDURE DIVISION.
      PARA-1.
*                         PROGA1____
      IDENTIFICATION DIVISION.
      PROGRAM-ID. PROGA1.
      .............
      PROCEDURE DIVISION.
      PARA-A1-1.

      END PROGRAM PROGA1.
*                         PROGA1____
*                         PROGA2____
      IDENTIFICATION DIVISION.
```

133

```
PROGRAM-ID. PROGA2.
..........
PROCEDURE DIVISION.
PARA-A2-1.

END PROGRAM PROGA2.
*                      PROGA2____
END PROGRAM MAIN.

*                      MAIN
```

To pass control to a nested program the CALL verb is used as with separately compiled programs. Parameters may also be used. A disadvantage of COBOL as compared with Pascal is that we cannot indent the COBOL program to reflect levels of nesting. All programs, whatever the level of nesting, must be entered in columns specified for areas A and B (see chapter 1).

The user should ensure that the installation supports nested programs before trying to use this facility, and should consult the manual to see whether any special instructions are required to compile a program that contains calls to nested programs. MicroFocus COBOL for example requires a compiler directive. To compile a program MAIN contained in a file Main.CBL using MicroFocus COBOL we would enter the command

```
COBOL MAIN NESTCALL
```

Failure to append the directive NESTCALL produces a compilation error and a misleading error message.

The first example (14.1) shows the use of a nested program to accept input from the keyboard. The calling program uses parameters to pass in the prompt message, the type (alphabetic, numeric or alphanumeric) and, in case of numeric, the range allowed. The program shown in example 14.1 allows us to test each type of entry by making a sequence of calls to the nested program and displaying the reply received from the program. It will be noticed that to reduce repetition of the parameters the CALL statement is placed in a separate paragraph. It should also be noted that the security of the calling program is increased by designating four of the parameters BY CONTENT (see chapter 13).

The nested program KEYBD uses a loop to accept and validate user input until valid entry has been entered. This is then passed back via Reply to WS-REPLY in the main program. In order to validate numeric entries, spaces are converted to zeros using the INSPECT verb.

```
IDENTIFICATION DIVISION.
PROGRAM-ID. MAIN.

DATA DIVISION.
WORKING-STORAGE SECTION.
    01  WS-PROMPT          PIC X(16).
    01  WS-REPLY           PIC X(20).
    01  WS-TYPE            PIC  X.
    01  WS-UPPER-LIMIT     PIC 9(6).
    01  WS-LOWER-LIMIT     PIC 9(6).

PROCEDURE DIVISION.
MAIN-PARA.
    MOVE "ENTER ITEM PRICE" TO WS-PROMPT.
    MOVE "N" TO WS-TYPE.
    MOVE 25 TO WS-LOWER-LIMIT.
    MOVE 1000 TO WS-UPPER-LIMIT.
    PERFORM CALL-KEYBOARD.
    DISPLAY WS-REPLY.
*   Tests numeric validation
    MOVE "Enter name" TO WS-PROMPT.
    MOVE "A" TO WS-TYPE.
    PERFORM CALL-KEYBOARD.
    DISPLAY WS-REPLY.
*   Tests alphabetic validation
    MOVE "Enter post code " TO WS-PROMPT.
    MOVE "P" TO WS-TYPE.
    PERFORM CALL-KEYBOARD.
    DISPLAY WS-REPLY.
*   Tests alphanumeric validation
    STOP RUN.

CALL-KEYBOARD.
    CALL "KEYBD" USING
                BY  CONTENT WS-PROMPT
                            WS-TYPE
                            WS-UPPER-LIMIT
                            WS-LOWER-LIMIT
                BY REFERENCE WS-REPLY.
* The nested program KEYBD begins on the next line
IDENTIFICATION DIVISION.
PROGRAM-ID. KEYBD IS INITIAL.

DATA DIVISION.
WORKING-STORAGE SECTION.
  01 REPLY-INDICATOR  PIC X
                VALUE "I".
     88 VALID-REPLY
                VALUE "V".
```

```
        LINKAGE SECTION.
            01  PROMPT-MESSAGE          PIC X(16).
            01  REPLY-TYPE              PIC X.
            01  UPPER-RANGE             PIC 9(6).
            01  LOWER-RANGE             PIC 9(6).
            01  REPLY                   PIC X(20).

        PROCEDURE DIVISION USING
                                    PROMPT-MESSAGE
                                    REPLY-TYPE
                                    UPPER-RANGE
                                    LOWER-RANGE
                                    REPLY.
    MAIN-PARA.
        PERFORM UNTIL VALID-REPLY
            DISPLAY PROMPT-MESSAGE WITH NO ADVANCING
            ACCEPT REPLY
            EVALUATE REPLY-TYPE
              WHEN "N"
                        INSPECT REPLY REPLACING ALL SPACES
                                                BY ZEROS
                        IF REPLY NUMERIC
                        THEN
                          IF REPLY >= LOWER-RANGE AND
                                    REPLY <= UPPER-RANGE
                          THEN
                            MOVE "V" TO REPLY-INDICATOR
                          ELSE DISPLAY REPLY "out of range : "
                                LOWER-RANGE " TO " UPPER-RANGE
                        ELSE
                            DISPLAY "NUMERIC Entry Required"
                        END-IF
                WHEN "A" IF REPLY ALPHABETIC
                        THEN
                            MOVE "V" TO REPLY-INDICATOR
                        ELSE
                            DISPLAY "Alphabetic entry required"
                        END-IF
                WHEN "P" MOVE "V" TO REPLY-INDICATOR
            END-EVALUATE
        END-PERFORM.

    END-PARA.
        EXIT PROGRAM.

    END PROGRAM KEYBD.
    * The previous line terminates the nested program.

    END PROGRAM MAIN.
```

Example 14.1 Calling a nested program, COBOL 85

It may be noted that the nested PROGRAM uses IS INITIAL to reinitialise the data item REPLY-INDICATOR.

We may now include a further example (14.2) which shows how we could 'hide' a table of integers within a nested program. At present the table is accessed by supplying the subscript and a code to indicate whether items are being added or retrieved. It would be easy to add operations to allow the table to be searched for the presence of an item. We could also readily amend it to allow the table to be initialised from a file and to write its state out to a file. The use of EVALUATE in the nested program, although not strictly necessary, makes the addition of further operations straightforward.

It should be noted that without the IS INITIAL the nested program maintains its state between calls in the same way as a separately compiled program.

```
        IDENTIFICATION DIVISION.
        PROGRAM-ID. MAIN.

        DATA DIVISION.
        WORKING-STORAGE SECTION.
            01  WS-LOCATION           PIC 999.
            01  WS-VALUE              PIC 9(9).
            01  WS-OP-CODE            PIC X.
            01  WS-DISPLAY-VALUE      PIC Z(8)9.

        PROCEDURE DIVISION.
        MAIN-PARA.
            MOVE 23 TO WS-LOCATION.
            MOVE "A" TO WS-OP-CODE.
            MOVE  2345 TO WS-VALUE.
            PERFORM CALL-LIST.
    *   Adds 2345 to location 23 in table
            MOVE 1 TO WS-LOCATION.
            MOVE "R" TO WS-OP-CODE.
            PERFORM CALL-LIST.
            MOVE WS-VALUE TO WS-DISPLAY-VALUE.
            DISPLAY WS-DISPLAY-VALUE.
    *   Retrieves and displays contents of location 1
            MOVE 23 TO WS-LOCATION.
            PERFORM CALL-LIST.
            MOVE WS-VALUE TO WS-DISPLAY-VALUE.
            DISPLAY WS-DISPLAY-VALUE.
```

```
    *   Retrieves contents of location 23
            STOP RUN.
        CALL-LIST.
            CALL "LIST" USING
                        WS-LOCATION
                        WS-OP-CODE
                        WS-VALUE.


    *  The nested program begins on the next line
       IDENTIFICATION DIVISION.
       PROGRAM-ID. LIST.
       DATA DIVISION.
       WORKING-STORAGE SECTION.
           01  LIST-OF-INTEGERS VALUE ZERO.
               03 WS-ITEM OCCURS 100   PIC 9(9).


       LINKAGE SECTION.
           01  INDX              PIC 999.
           01  IN-OUT-VALUE      PIC 9(9).
           01 OPERATION          PIC X.


       PROCEDURE DIVISION USING
                            INDX
                            OPERATION
                            IN-OUT-VALUE.

       MAIN-PARA.
           EVALUATE OPERATION
               WHEN "A" MOVE IN-OUT-VALUE TO WS-ITEM(INDX)
               WHEN "R" MOVE WS-ITEM(INDX) TO IN-OUT-VALUE
           END-EVALUATE.
       END-PARA.
           EXIT PROGRAM.
       END PROGRAM LIST.
    * The previous line terminates the nested program.

       END PROGRAM MAIN.
```

Example 14.2 Hiding a table in a nested program

We may now summarise the main features of nested programs.

1. Nested programs are added to the end of the Procedure Division and before the End-Program header of the program within which they are nested.

2. The same formatting rules apply to all programs whether nested or not.

3. Nested programs are similar in the following respects to separately compiled programs:

i) they are called using the CALL verb, followed by the program identifier in quotation marks;

ii) if accepting parameters they require a Linkage Section and a USING phrase appended to the Procedure Division header;

iii) they maintain their state between calls unless explicitly initialised or cancelled (see chapter 13);

iv) data-names within the nested program are local to the nested program;

v) data-names in a calling program are not visible to the nested program.

We must now investigate the rules that govern which program may call another, and finally the facility to declare global data.

14.2 Visibility of Nested Programs

COBOL 85 has rather complicated rules governing the visibility of nested programs. We will begin by refreshing the reader's memory about the rules which determine the visibility of nested procedures within Pascal (example 14.3), and we will then compare these with the rules for COBOL 85. The

```
PROGRAM Main (Input,Output);
  PROCEDURE A;
     PROCEDURE A1;
     BEGIN
(* A  and A1 - ( recursive) may be called from here*)
     END;  (*A1*)

     PROCEDURE A2;
     BEGIN
(*A and A2 - (recursive ) and A1 may be called from here*)
     END;  (*A2*)
   BEGIN
(* A - (recursive), A1 and A2 may be called from here *)
   END; (*A*)
BEGIN
(* Procedure A may be called from here*)
END; (*MAIN*)
```

Example 14.3 Visibility of procedures in Pascal

reader will now be aware that we are not strictly comparing like with like; a Pascal procedure and a nested COBOL program have different properties, although it is possible to make a COBOL program behave like a Pascal procedure by using the CANCEL statement or the INITIAL phrase (see chapter 13), and global and local data names (see section 14.3).

A comparable situation for COBOL 85 is illustrated in example 14.4 below. It should immediately be noted that no recursive calls are permitted. This program may be entered and executed. The output it produces should be easy to work out.

```
IDENTIFICATION DIVISION.
PROGRAM-ID. MAIN.

PROCEDURE DIVISION.
    DISPLAY "A Call to PROGA may be made from here".
    CALL "PROGA".
    STOP RUN.
IDENTIFICATION DIVISION.
PROGRAM-ID. PROGA.

PROCEDURE DIVISION.
* Program PROGA nested within MAIN
    DISPLAY "PROGA: PROGA1 and PROGA2 may be called".
    CALL "PROGA1".
    CALL "PROGA2".
EXIT-PARA.
    EXIT PROGRAM.

IDENTIFICATION DIVISION.
PROGRAM-ID. PROGA1.
PROCEDURE DIVISION.
* Program PROGA1 nested within PROGA
    DISPLAY " PROGA1  : No calls  possible".
EXIT-PARA.
    EXIT PROGRAM.
END PROGRAM PROGA1.

IDENTIFICATION DIVISION
PROGRAM-ID. PROGA2.
PROCEDURE DIVISION.
* Program PROGA2 nested within PROGA
    DISPLAY " No calls are possible from PROGA2".
EXIT-PARA.
    EXIT PROGRAM.
END PROGRAM PROGA2.

END PROGRAM PROGA.

END PROGRAM MAIN.
```

Example 14.4 Visibility of nested programs in COBOL 85

It should be noted that a program may not call another at the same level of nesting unless a COMMON phrase is appended to the program name of the called program. In example 14.4, therefore, PROGA2 may not call PROGA1. Example 14.5 shows how program PROGA1 could be declared as COMMON, which would allow PROGA2 and any programs nested within PROGA2 to call PROGA1. Any program nested within PROGA1 may still not call PROGA1, because of the no-recursion rule, and it is also illegal to make PROGA1 and PROGA2 mutually recursive.

```
IDENTIFICATION DIVISION.
PROGRAM-ID. MAIN.

PROCEDURE DIVISION.
        DISPLAY "A Call to PROGA may be made from here".
        CALL "PROGA".
        STOP RUN.
IDENTIFICATION DIVISION.
PROGRAM-ID. PROGA.

PROCEDURE DIVISION.
* Program PROGA nested within MAIN
        DISPLAY "PROGA: PROGA1 and PROGA2 may be called".
        CALL "PROGA1".
        CALL "PROGA2".
EXIT-PARA.
        EXIT PROGRAM.

IDENTIFICATION DIVISION.
PROGRAM-ID. PROGA1 IS COMMON.
PROCEDURE DIVISION.
* Program PROGA1 nested within PROGA
        DISPLAY " PROGA1  : No calls  possible".
EXIT-PARA.
        EXIT PROGRAM.
END PROGRAM PROGA1.

IDENTIFICATION DIVISION.
PROGRAM-ID. PROGA2.
PROCEDURE DIVISION.
* Program PROGA2 nested within PROGA
        DISPLAY "PROGA2: PROGA1 may be called: Is Common".
        CALL "PROGA1"
EXIT-PARA.
        EXIT PROGRAM.
END PROGRAM PROGA2.

END PROGRAM PROGA.

END PROGRAM MAIN.
```

Example 14.5 Use of COMMON phrase in COBOL 85

14.3   Local and Global Data-names

In Pascal, the scope rules mean that names declared in a block are visible in all blocks nested within that block unless they are redefined.

```
PROGRAM Main (Input,Output);
   VAR X,Y: Integer;
   PROCEDURE A;
   VAR X:Real;
   BEGIN
(* Global Y is visible here; X has been locally redefined*)
   END;(*A*)
   BEGIN

   END;(*MAIN*)
```

Example 14.6 Visibility of identifiers in Pascal

In example 14.6 the variables X and Y have been declared as integers in the outer block. Y is visible in the nested block, but X has been redefined and so only the local X is visible.

One of the deficiencies of COBOL 74 is that all data within a program is global; the only way to localise data is to use separately compiled programs. The introduction of nested programs has remedied this deficiency. Data names declared in a nested program are local to that program, in the same way as data declared in a separately compiled program. It is now possible, however, to create global File Descriptions and 01 level records. A global identifier in COBOL 85 is visible in all nested programs in the same way as in Pascal. The difference is that the default is local; a data-name declared in an outer program cannot be referenced in a nested program unless it is explicitly declared as GLOBAL. Example 14.7 provides a simple illustration of the workings of the global facility, while examples 14.8 and 14.9 provide slightly fuller illustrations of the use of a global file description and a global table.

In example 14.7 the level 1 record ANY-REC is declared as global; this automatically means that all subordinate data items and condition names are global. The reader should be able to work out the output that would be produced by the program in example 14.7. The global data item ANY-REC is altered in the nested program, so that on return to the main program the new values given in the nested program will be displayed.

```
IDENTIFICATION DIVISION.
PROGRAM-ID. MAIN.
DATA DIVISION.
WORKING-STORAGE SECTION.
    01 ANY-REC  IS GLOBAL.
        03  WS-NAME          PIC X(20).
        03  WS-DATE-OF-BIRTH PIC 9(6).


PROCEDURE DIVISION.
MAIN-1.
    DISPLAY "In Main Program".
    MOVE "JAMES SMITH" TO WS-NAME.
    MOVE 220959 TO WS-DATE-OF-BIRTH.
    DISPLAY ANY-REC.
    CALL "PROGA".
    DISPLAY "In Main Program".
    DISPLAY ANY-REC.
    STOP RUN.


IDENTIFICATION DIVISION.
PROGRAM-ID. PROGA.


PROCEDURE DIVISION.
PARA-A1.
    DISPLAY "PROGA"
    DISPLAY " ANY-REC visible".
    DISPLAY ANY-REC.
    DISPLAY "WS-NAME visible".
    MOVE "JOHN BROWN" TO WS-NAME.
    DISPLAY " WS-DATE-OF-BIRTH visible".
    MOVE 021024 TO WS-DATE-OF-BIRTH
EXIT-PARA.
    EXIT PROGRAM.


END PROGRAM PROGA.


END PROGRAM MAIN.
```

Example 14.7 Use of the GLOBAL phrase, COBOL 85

```
IDENTIFICATION DIVISION.
PROGRAM-ID. MAIN.
ENVIRONMENT DIVISION.
INPUT-OUTPUT SECTION.
FILE-CONTROL.
    SELECT  DATA1
    ASSIGN TO   implementor-name
    ORGANIZATION IS SEQUENTIAL
    ACCESS MODE IS SEQUENTIAL.
DATA DIVISION.
FILE SECTION.
FD  DATA1 IS GLOBAL.
 01 PERSON-REC IS GLOBAL.
      03 P-NAME           PIC X(20).
      03 DATE-OF-BIRTH    PIC 9(6).

WORKING-STORAGE SECTION.
 01 FILE-STATE  IS GLOBAL   PIC X
           VALUE "C".
PROCEDURE DIVISION.
MAIN-1.
    MOVE "W.R. Bloggs" TO P-NAME.
    MOVE 201257 TO DATE-OF-BIRTH.
    CALL "WFILE".
    CLOSE DATA1.
    MOVE "C" TO FILE-STATE.
    .........
    STOP RUN.

IDENTIFICATION DIVISION.
PROGRAM-ID WFILE.

PROCEDURE DIVISION.
WFILE-1.
    EVALUATE FILE-STATE
        WHEN "C"   OPEN EXTEND DATA1
                   WRITE PERSON-REC
                   MOVE "E" TO FILE-STATE
        WHEN "E"   WRITE PERSON-REC
        WHEN OTHER
            DISPLAY "INVALID REQUEST TO WRITE TO FILE"
    END-EVALUATE.
EXIT-PARA.
    EXIT PROGRAM.

END PROGRAM WFILE.

END PROGRAM MAIN.
```

Example 14.8 Use of a GLOBAL file

The program illustrated in example 14.8 adds a single record to a global file by calling a nested program. It only does so if the file state indicates that the program is open for extension, or the file is closed. In the latter case it opens the file for extension before writing a record. It would be possible to add other programs to perform similar operations on the file. If, for example, the program required to read records from the file, then another program would be written to open the file for input and perform a read. This program would be similar to WFILE, with a safeguard which ensured that it did nothing unless FILE-STATE indicated that the file was closed or open for input.

Study Guide

This chapter has covered nested programs, global declarations, and the rules for the visibility of nested subprograms. The reader is recommended to make notes on each of these topics.

Practical Exercises

1. Amend example 14.8 by adding a nested program which reads a record sequentially from the file.
2. Alter the program in example 14.8 to make it a separately compiled module called externally; the main program should offer the user the facility to read, write, open, or close a file, and may call nested programs to carry out the operations required.

Appendix 1   Glossary

ALPHABETIC DATA ITEM
A data item which may contain only alphabetic characters and spaces.

ALPHANUMERIC DATA ITEM
A data item which may contain any characters from the computer's character set.

AREA A
Columns 8-11 of source program line, used for division, section and paragraph headings, and for level 1 record declarations.

AREA B
Usually columns 12-72 of the source line, used for the declaration of subordinate data items and for statements.

ARITHMETIC OPERATORS

```
+       -
*       /
** (exponentiation)
```

ASSIGNMENT
Operation which assigns the result of an expression to a variable. No assignment operator exists in COBOL, but assignment may be achieved by using the COMPUTE verb for arithmetic expressions, and the MOVE verb to assign single values.

BY CONTENT
Mode of parameter passing which prevents alterations to the contents of a parameter from being passed back to the calling program. Not supported in COBOL 74.

BY REFERENCE
Mode of parameter passing which allows alterations to the contents of a parameter to be received by the calling program. The default parameter passing mode in COBOL.

CALLED PROGRAM
A subprogram which is invoked by a CALL statement. In COBOL 74 this may only be a separately compiled program, but in COBOL 85 it may also be a program nested within the calling program.

CALLING PROGRAM
A program which uses a CALL statement to pass control to another program.

CLASS CONDITION
Used to establish if the contents of a data item are of a given type, eg Alphabetic, Numeric.

COBOL 74
The 1974 ANSI COBOL standard.

COBOL 85
The 1985 ANSI COBOL standard.

CONDITION NAME
A name associated with a data item, defined using a level 88 declaration. The condition is true when one of the values assigned to the condition name matches the value in the associated data item.

CONTROL ABSTRACTION
Language facilities which hide the low-level changes to program flow necessary to realise selection and repetition.

DIVISION
The four main units of a COBOL program. Each consists of a name and a body. They are Identification, Environment, Data and Procedure Divisions.

DYNAMIC ACCESS
Access mode used for indexed and relative files which allows both sequential and random access to records within the file.

EDITING CHARACTERS
Characters inserted in picture strings of items used for display purposes only:

```
Z    zero suppression      £    currency symbol
.    decimal point         ,    comma (inserted in large numbers)
+    plus                   -    minus
```

ELEMENTARY DATA ITEM
A data item which has no subordinate items.

FIGURATIVE CONSTANT
Reserved words used to represent heavily used constants, eg SPACE, ZERO.

FILE DESCRIPTION
The entry in the File Section of the Data Division beginning with FD.

GLOBAL DATA
Facility available in COBOL 85 which allows a file or data item to be visible to programs nested within the program in which the global item is declared.

GROUP DATA ITEM
A data item which has no picture string but has one or more subordinate items, of which at least one must be an elementary item.

INDEX
A special data item used to access a table; it contains a binary value which represents the byte displacement from the beginning of the table.

INDEXED FILE
A file in which each record is uniquely identified by a key field, and accessed using an index or indexes maintained by the system.

KEY WORD
A reserved word which must be used when the construct of which it is a part is selected, eg IF is a key word, THEN is optional.

LEVEL NUMBER
Single or double digit numbers which either identify the level of an item within a record hierarchy (range 1..49) or indicate a special property: level 88 denotes a condition name, level 66 may be used to rename an area of memory, and 77 may be used to define a stand-alone elementary item.

LITERAL
A string of characters.

LOGICAL OPERATORS
Reserved words AND, OR, NOT, used to connect or negate simple conditions.

NESTED PROGRAM
A facility available in COBOL 85 which allows a called program to be embedded in the calling program. The end of each called and calling program is denoted by an end program header, which consists of END PROGRAM, followed by the program-name. A nested program has similar attributes to a separately compiled program except that it may access global data declared in a surrounding program.

NUMERIC DATA ITEM

An item which consists only of digits and no more than one sign, and may be used in calculations.

NUMERIC EDITED DATA ITEM

A numeric item used for display purposes only, which includes special editing characters for the display of signs, zero suppression and decimal point.

NON-NUMERIC LITERAL

A character string enclosed by quotation marks.

NUMERIC LITERAL

A sequence of up to 18 digits, preceded by an optional sign; it may include one decimal point, and if so must contain at least one digit to the right of the point.

PARAGRAPH

A subdivision of either a section or a division. In the Procedure Division it consists of a user-defined name followed by a sequence of statements.

PARAMETER PASSING

Passing of values between calling and called programs. COBOL 74 supports passing by reference (variable parameters in Pascal). COBOL 85 allows a programmer to select whether an actual parameter is to be passed BY REFERENCE or BY CONTENT (a value parameter in Pascal).

PICTURE STRING

Sequence of characters following reserved word PIC or PICTURE, which determine the range of values that may be stored in an elementary data item.

PROCEDURAL ABSTRACTION

Hierarchical design and implementation method. In Pascal this may be realised using procedures and functions, in COBOL it may be realised using the PERFORM verb to call paragraphs or sections.

PROGRAM NAME

A user-defined name defined in the Identification Division. This name is used to call a separately compiled or a nested program.

QUALIFIED DATA NAME

A data name uniquely identified by its full path name within the record hierarchy in which it occurs. This is achieved by using OF or IN.

RANDOM ACCESS

Access mode used with indexed and relative files to allow records to be accessed in any order by specifying the key value of the record required.

RECORD
A level 1 data item, which may be either elementary or grouped.

RELATIONAL OPERATORS
Reserved words or special characters used to form a relational condition.

```
GREATER THAN              >
LESS THAN                 <
EQUAL TO                  =
```

Each may be preceded by NOT. COBOL 85 provides additional operators.

```
GREATER THAN OR EQUAL TO   >=
LESS THAN OR EQUAL TO      <=
```

RELATIVE FILE
A file in which a record may be uniquely identified by its ordinal position within the file.

REPETITION
Statement which is capable of executing more than once. Pascal provides While, Repeat and For statements. COBOL 74 provides no in-line repetitive statements, but provides the PERFORM UNTIL and the PERFORM VARYING for out-of-line repetition. COBOL 85 allows in-line use of the PERFORM verb.

RESERVED WORD
A word which has a special meaning in COBOL and cannot be selected as a user-defined word.

RUN UNIT
One or more programs combined into a single executable unit.

SCOPE TERMINATOR
Member of the set of reserved words introduced into COBOL 85 which denote the end of the scope of a statement. Scope terminators are formed by appending the statement name to END-, eg END-READ.

SECTION
A subunit of a COBOL Division, which consists of a section header, eg WORKING-STORAGE SECTION, and may be further subdivided into paragraphs. If a Division is subdivided into sections, then all paragraphs must be contained within sections.

SELECTION
Structured statement which allows the execution of one path from a number of alternatives depending on a condition. Pascal provides If Else and Case statements. COBOL provides an IF ELSE statement. In addition COBOL 85 provides an EVALUATE statement which is similar to the Pascal Case statement.

SEPARATELY COMPILED PROGRAM
A program which is either the subject or object of a CALL statement but is compiled separately from its called or calling programs.

SEQUENTIAL ACCESS
Access mode which may be used for all file organisations. In the case of sequential files it allows records to be accessed in the temporal order in which they have been placed on the file. In the case of indexed and relative files it allows records to be retrieved in key order only.

SEQUENTIAL FILE
A file in which records are stored in the order in which they are placed on the file.

SIZE ERROR CONDITION
Loss of significant digits when a value to be stored exceeds the size of the data item; this may be detected by using the ON SIZE ERROR phrase.

STATEMENT
A Procedure Division entry commencing with a verb.

SUBORDINATE DATA ITEM
A data item which is contained in a group item.

SUBSCRIPT
A data-name or numeric literal which identifies a particular element in a table.

TABLE
A data structure which contains an iteration of data items defined using an OCCURS clause.

USER-DEFINED NAME
A word supplied by the programmer to define program names, files, data items and paragraph names, which must not be drawn from the list of reserved words.

VALUE CLAUSE
Clause used to assign an initial value to a data item or a constant set of values to a condition name.

VERB
A key word used to begin each Procedure Division statement.

Appendix 2 COBOL Reserved Words

*Words preceded by * are available in COBOL 85 only.*

ACCEPT	ACCESS	ADD
ADVANCING	AFTER	ALL
*ALPHABET	ALPHABETIC	*ALPHABETIC-LOWER
*ALPHABETIC-UPPER	*ALPHANUMERIC	*ALPHANUMERIC-EDITED
ALSO	ALTER	ALTERNATE
AND	*ANY	ARE
AREA	AREAS	ASCENDING
ASSIGN	AT	AUTHOR
BEFORE	*BINARY	BLANK
BLOCK	BOTTOM	BY
CALL	CANCEL	CD
CF	CH	CHARACTER
CHARACTERS	CLASS	CLOCK-UNITS
CLOSE	CODE	CODE-SET
COLLATING	COLUMN	COMMA
COMMON	COMMUNICATION	COMP
COMPUTATIONAL	COMPUTE	CONFIGURATION
CONTAINS	*CONTENT	CONTINUE
CONTROL	CONTROLS	CONVERTING
COPY	CORR	CORRESPONDING
COUNT	CURRENCY	
DATA	DATE	DATE-COMPILED
DATE-WRITTEN	DAY	*DAY-OF-WEEK
DE	DEBUG-CONTENTS	DEBUG-ITEM
DEBUG-LINE	DEBUG-NAME	DEBUG-SUB-1
DEBUG-SUB-2	DEBUG-SUB-3	DEBUGGING
DECIMAL-POINT	DECLARATIVES	DELETE
DELIMITED	DELIMITER	DEPENDING
DESCENDING	DESTINATION	DETAIL

DISABLE   DISPLAY   DIVIDE
DIVISION   DOWN   DUPLICATES
DYNAMIC

EGI   ELSE   EMI
ENABLE   END   *END-ADD
*END-CALL   *END-COMPUTE   *END-DELETE
*END-DIVIDE   *END-EVALUATE   *END-IF
*END-MULTIPLY   END-OF-PAGE   *END-PERFORM
*END-READ   *END-RECEIVE   *END-RETURN
*END-REWRITE   *END-SEARCH   *END-START
*END-STRING   *END-SUBTRACT   *END-UNSTRING
*END-WRITE   ENTER   ENVIRONMENT
EOP   EQUAL   ERROR
ESI   *EVALUATE   EVERY
EXCEPTION   EXIT   EXTEND
EXTERNAL

*FALSE   FD   FILE
FILE-CONTROL   FILLER   FINAL
FIRST   FOOTING   FOR
FROM

GENERATE   GIVING   *GLOBAL
GO   GREATER   GROUP

HEADING   HIGH-VALUE   HIGH-VALUES

I-O   I-O-CONTROL   IDENTIFICATION
IF   IN   INDEX
INDEXED   INDICATE   INITIAL
*INITIALIZE   INITIATE   INPUT
INPUT-OUTPUT   INSPECT   INSTALLATION
INTO   INVALID   IS

JUST   JUSTIFIED

KEY

LABEL	LAST	LEADING
LEFT	LENGTH	LESS
LIMIT	LIMITS	LINAGE
LINAGE-COUNTER	LINE	LINE-COUNTER
LINES	LINKAGE	LOCK
LOW-VALUE	LOW-VALUES	

MEMORY	MERGE	MESSAGE
MODE	MODULES	MOVE
MULTIPLE	MULTIPLY	

NATIVE	NEGATIVE	NEXT
NO	NOT	NUMBER
NUMERIC	*NUMERIC-EDITED	

OBJECT-COMPUTER	OCCURS	OF
OFF	OMITTED	ON
OPEN	OPTIONAL	OR
*ORDER	ORGANIZATION	*OTHER
OUTPUT	OVERFLOW	

*PACKED-DECIMAL	*PADDING	PAGE
PAGE-COUNTER	PERFORM	PF
PH	PIC	PICTURE
PLUS	POINTER	*POSITION
POSITIVE	PRINTING	PROCEDURE
PROCEDURES	PROCEED	PROGRAM
PROGRAM-ID	*PURGE	

QUEUE	QUOTE	QUOTES

RANDOM	RD	READ
RECEIVE	RECORD	RECORDS
REDEFINES	REEL	*REFERENCE
REFERENCES	RELATIVE	RELEASE
REMAINDER	REMOVAL	RENAMES
*REPLACE	REPLACING	REPORT
REPORTING	REPORTS	RERUN
RESERVE	RESET	RETURN
REVERSED	REWIND	REWRITE

RF	RH	RIGHT
ROUNDED	RUN	

SAME	SD	SEARCH
SECTION	SECURITY	SEGMENT
SEGMENT-LIMIT	SELECT	SEND
SENTENCE	SEPARATE	SEQUENCE
SEQUENTIAL	SET	SIGN
SIZE	SORT	SORT-MERGE
SOURCE	SOURCE-COMPUTER	SPACE
SPACES	SPECIAL-NAMES	STANDARD
STANDARD-1	*STANDARD-2	START
STATUS	STOP	STRING
SUB-QUEUE-1	SUB-QUEUE-2	SUB-QUEUE-3
SUBTRACT	SUM	SUPPRESS
SYMBOLIC	SYNC	SYNCHRONIZED

TABLE	TALLYING	TAPE
TERMINAL	TERMINATE	*TEST
TEXT	THAN	*THEN
THROUGH	THRU	TIME
TIMES	TO	TOP
TRAILING	*TRUE	TYPE

UNIT	UNSTRING	UNTIL
UP	UPON	USAGE
USE	USING	

VALUE	VALUES	VARYING

WHEN	WITH	WORDS
WORKING-STORAGE	WRITE	

ZERO	ZEROES	ZEROS

Appendix 3   Main COBOL Statements

This appendix provides a guide to the syntax of the main COBOL statements. First an introduction is provided to the meta language used to define COBOL syntax. The reader should note that the rules given are sometimes simplified; this appendix does not claim to define a COBOL standard or to replace a manual.
Language features marked with a * are available in COBOL 85 only.

1. COBOL MetaLanguage

The following symbols are used:
[   ] denotes optional elements;
{   } one of the options must be selected
{| |} one or more of the elements enclosed must be selected
... indicates that an element may be selected more than once
Underlined uppercase words are key words and must be included when the element of which they form part is selected. Other uppercase words are optional.
   Lower case words are used to indicate the type of entity the user must supply , eg identifier, literal.
   As an example we may take the following definition of the Program-Id entry for COBOL 85:

PROGRAM-ID   identifier   [IS { |COMMON| }   PROGRAM]
                                  { |INITIAL| }

Given the above rule, each of the following is syntactically correct:

        PROGRAM-ID ANYPROG.

        PROGRAM-ID ANYPROG INITIAL.
        PROGRAM-ID ANYPROG INITIAL PROGRAM.
        PROGRAM-ID ANYPROG IS INITIAL.
        PROGRAM-ID ANYPROG IS INITIAL PROGRAM.

```
PROGRAM-ID ANYPROG COMMON.
PROGRAM-ID ANYPROG COMMON PROGRAM.
PROGRAM-ID ANYPROG IS COMMON.
PROGRAM-ID ANYPROG IS COMMON PROGRAM.

PROGRAM-ID ANYPROG INITIAL COMMON.
PROGRAM-ID ANYPROG IS INITIAL COMMON.
PROGRAM-ID ANYPROG INITIAL COMMON PROGRAM.
PROGRAM-ID ANYPROG IS INITIAL COMMON PROGRAM.
```

2. COBOL Statements

2.1 ACCEPT

ACCEPT identifier [FROM mnemonic-name]

ACCEPT identifier FROM $\begin{Bmatrix} \text{DATE} \\ \text{DAY-OF-WEEK*} \\ \text{TIME} \\ \text{DAY} \end{Bmatrix}$

2.2 ADD

(i) ADD $\begin{Bmatrix} \text{identifier} \\ \text{literal} \end{Bmatrix}$ ... TO { identifier [ROUNDED] }...

      [ON SIZE ERROR imperative-statement]

      [NOT ON SIZE ERROR imperative-statement] *

  [END-ADD] *

(ii) ADD $\begin{Bmatrix} \text{identifier} \\ \text{literal} \end{Bmatrix}$ ... TO $\begin{Bmatrix} \text{identifier} \\ \text{literal} \end{Bmatrix}$

     GIVING {identifier [ROUNDED]} ...

      [ON SIZE ERROR imperative-statement]

      [NOT ON SIZE ERROR imperative-statement] *

  [END-ADD] *

2.3 CALL

```
CALL  { identifier* }
      { literal     }

      [ USING  { [BY REFERENCE ] *  {identifier} ... }... ]
               { BY CONTENT *      {identifier}    ... }

[END-CALL]*
```

Note: The 74 rule is:

```
CALL  literal  [USING identifier ...  ]
```

2.4 CLOSE

```
CLOSE filename ...
```

2.5 COMPUTE

```
COMPUTE   {identifier [ROUNDED] } ...   = arithmetic-expression

[ON SIZE ERROR imperative-statement]

[NOT ON SIZE ERROR imperative-statement] *

[END-COMPUTE]*
```

2.6 DELETE

```
DELETE  filename

      [INVALID KEY imperative-statement]

      [NOT INVALID KEY imperative-statement]*

[END-DELETE]*
```

2.7 DISPLAY

DISPLAY $\left\{ \begin{array}{l} \text{literal} \\ \text{identifier} \end{array} \right\}$ ... [UPON mnemonic-name]

2.8 DIVIDE

(i) DIVIDE $\left\{ \begin{array}{l} \text{identifier} \\ \text{literal} \end{array} \right\}$ INTO {identifier [ROUNDED]} ...

       [ON SIZE ERROR imperative-statement]

       [NOT ON SIZE ERROR imperative-statement]*

  [END-DIVIDE]*

(ii) DIVIDE $\left\{ \begin{array}{l} \text{identifier} \\ \text{literal} \end{array} \right\}$ INTO $\left\{ \begin{array}{l} \text{identifier} \\ \text{literal} \end{array} \right\}$

      GIVING {identifier [ROUNDED]} ...

      [ON SIZE ERROR imperative-statement]

      [NOT ON SIZE ERROR imperative-statement]*

  [END-DIVIDE]*

(iii) DIVIDE $\left\{ \begin{array}{l} \text{identifier} \\ \text{literal} \end{array} \right\}$ BY $\left\{ \begin{array}{l} \text{identifier} \\ \text{literal} \end{array} \right\}$

     GIVING { identifier [ROUNDED] } ...

      [ON SIZE ERROR imperative-statement]

      [NOT ON SIZE ERROR imperative-statement]*

  [END-DIVIDE] *

(iv) <u>DIVIDE</u>   { identifier }   <u>INTO</u>   { identifier }
     { literal   }   { literal   }

      <u>GIVING</u>   identifier [<u>ROUNDED</u>]
               <u>REMAINDER</u>   identifier

        [ON <u>SIZE</u> <u>ERROR</u> imperative-statement]

        [<u>NOT</u> ON <u>SIZE</u> <u>ERROR</u> imperative-statement]*

    [<u>END-DIVIDE</u>]*

(v) <u>DIVIDE</u>   { identifier }   <u>BY</u>   { identifier }
    { literal   }   { literal   }

      <u>GIVING</u>   identifier [<u>ROUNDED</u>]
               <u>REMAINDER</u>   identifier

        [ON <u>SIZE</u> <u>ERROR</u> imperative-statement]

        [<u>NOT</u> ON <u>SIZE</u> <u>ERROR</u> imperative-statement]*

    [<u>END-DIVIDE</u>]*

2.9 EVALUATE *

<u>EVALUATE</u>   { identifier }   [{ identifier }   ]
           { literal   }   [<u>ALSO</u> { literal   }   ] ...
           { expression }   { expression }
           { <u>TRUE</u>   }   { <u>TRUE</u>   }
           { <u>FALSE</u>   }   { <u>FALSE</u>   }

{<u>WHEN</u>   { <u>ANY</u>   }
        { condition   }
        { <u>TRUE</u>   }
        { <u>FALSE</u>   }
        {   }
        { [<u>NOT</u>] { identifier } [{<u>THROUGH</u>} [identifier]] }
        {   { literal   } [{<u>THRU</u>   } [literal   ]] }
        {   { arith-expn } [[arith-expn]] }

```
        ⎧         ANY                                                    ⎫
        ⎪         condition                                              ⎪
        ⎪         TRUE                                                   ⎪
        ⎪         FALSE                                                  ⎪
[ALSO   ⎨                                                                ⎬  ] ...
        ⎪        ⎧ identifier ⎫   ⎡ ⎧ THROUGH⎫  ⎧ identifier ⎫ ⎤         ⎪
        ⎪  [NOT] ⎨ literal    ⎬   ⎢ ⎨         ⎬  ⎨ literal    ⎬ ⎥         ⎪
        ⎩        ⎩ arith-expn ⎭   ⎣ ⎩ THRU    ⎭  ⎩ arith-expn ⎭ ⎦         ⎭
```

```
                              imperative-statement}      ...
             [WHEN OTHER  imperative-statement]
```

```
   [END-EVALUATE]
```

Note that EVALUATE is supported in the 85 standard only.

2.10 EXIT PROGRAM

```
     EXIT PROGRAM
```

2.11 IF

```
     IF condition
         THEN*  {statement}  ...
             [ELSE  {statement}  ... ]
     [END-IF]*
```

2.12 MOVE

```
     MOVE  ⎧ identifier ⎫     TO  {identifier}  ...
           ⎨ literal    ⎬
           ⎩            ⎭
```

2.13 MULTIPLY

```
(i)   MULTIPLY ⎧ identifier⎫  BY  {identifier[ROUNDED]}  ...
               ⎨ literal    ⎬·
               ⎩            ⎭

      [ON SIZE ERROR imperative-statement]

      [NOT ON SIZE ERROR imperative-statement]*

      [END-MULTIPLY]*
```

```
(ii)  MULTIPLY   ⎧ identifier ⎫    BY   ⎧ identifier ⎫
                 ⎨ literal     ⎬        ⎨ literal     ⎬
                 ⎩             ⎭        ⎩             ⎭

      GIVING   {identifier [ROUNDED]}  ...
```

[ON <u>SIZE</u> <u>ERROR</u> imperative-statement]

[<u>NOT</u> ON <u>SIZE</u> <u>ERROR</u> imperative-statement]*

[<u>END-MULTIPLY</u>]*

2.14 OPEN

<u>OPEN</u> $\left\{ \begin{array}{ll} \underline{INPUT} & \{filename\} \ \ldots \\ \underline{OUTPUT} & \{filename\} \ \ldots \\ \underline{I-O} & \{filename\} \ \ldots \\ \underline{EXTEND} & \{filename\} \ \ldots \end{array} \right\}$ ...

2.15 PERFORM (Out of line)

(i)   <u>PERFORM</u> procedure-name

(ii)   <u>PERFORM</u> procedure-name <u>UNTIL</u> condition

(iii) <u>PERFORM</u> procedure-name

$\left[\text{WITH } \underline{TEST} \quad \left\{ \begin{array}{ll} \underline{BEFORE} & * \\ \underline{AFTER} & * \end{array} \right\} \right] \underline{UNTIL}$ condition

(iv)   <u>PERFORM</u> procedure-name

$\left[\text{WITH } \underline{TEST} \quad \left\{ \begin{array}{ll} \underline{BEFORE} & * \\ \underline{AFTER} & * \end{array} \right\} \right]$

$\underline{VARYING} \quad \{identifier\} \quad \underline{FROM} \quad \left\{ \begin{array}{l} identifier \\ literal \end{array} \right\}$

$\underline{BY} \left\{ \begin{array}{l} identifier \\ literal \end{array} \right\} \quad \underline{UNTIL} \ condition$

2.16 PERFORM (in-line) *

(i)   <u>PERFORM</u> imperative-statement
      [<u>END-PERFORM</u>]

(ii) <u>PERFORM</u>

$$\left[\text{WITH } \underline{\text{TEST}} \quad \left\{ \begin{array}{l} \underline{\text{BEFORE}} \\ \underline{\text{AFTER}} \end{array} \right\} \right]$$

<u>UNTIL</u> condition

imperative-statement
[<u>END-PERFORM</u>]

(iii) <u>PERFORM</u>

$$\left[\text{WITH } \underline{\text{TEST}} \quad \left\{ \begin{array}{l} \underline{\text{BEFORE}} \\ \underline{\text{AFTER}} \end{array} \right\} \right]$$

<u>VARYING</u>   {identifier}   <u>FROM</u> $\left\{ \begin{array}{l} \text{identifier} \\ \text{literal} \end{array} \right\}$

<u>BY</u> $\left\{ \begin{array}{l} \text{identifier} \\ \text{literal} \end{array} \right\}$

<u>UNTIL</u>   condition

imperative-statement
[<u>END-PERFORM</u>]

2.17 READ

(i)   <u>READ</u> filename   RECORD   [<u>INTO</u> identifier]

[<u>KEY</u> IS identifier]

[<u>INVALID</u> KEY imperative statement]

[<u>NOT</u> <u>INVALID</u> KEY imperative-statement]*

[<u>END-READ</u>]*

(ii)   <u>READ</u> filename [<u>NEXT</u>] RECORD   [<u>INTO</u> identifier]

[AT <u>END</u> imperative-statement]

[<u>NOT</u> AT <u>END</u> imperative-statement]*

[<u>END-READ</u>]*

2.18 REWRITE

```
REWRITE record-name   [FROM identifier]

        [INVALID KEY imperative-statement]

        [NOT INVALID KEY imperative-statement]*

    [END-REWRITE]*
```

2.19 SEARCH

```
(1) SEARCH identifier  [ VARYING { identifier  } ]
                                 { index-name }
            [AT END imperative-statement]

        {WHEN condition        {imperative-statement}} ...

    [END-SEARCH]*
```

```
(2) SEARCH ALL identifier

        [AT END imperative-statement]

    WHEN ⎧ identifier { IS EQUAL TO } { identifier            } ⎫
         ⎪            { IS =         } { literal               } ⎪
         ⎨                            { arithmetic-expression  } ⎬
         ⎪                                                       ⎪
         ⎩ condition-name                                        ⎭

    ⎡ AND ⎧ identifier { IS EQUAL TO } { identifier           } ⎫ ⎤
    ⎢     ⎪            { IS =         } { literal              } ⎪ ⎥ ..
    ⎢     ⎨                            { arithmetic-expression} ⎬ ⎥
    ⎢     ⎪                                                     ⎪ ⎥
    ⎣     ⎩ condition-name                                      ⎭ ⎦

            imperative-statement

    [END-SEARCH]*
```

2.20 SET

```
SET  { index-name }  ...  TO  { index-name }
     { identifier  }           { identifier }
                               { integer    }

SET  {index-name}  ...  { UP BY   }  { identifier }
                        { DOWN BY }  { integer    }
```

2.21 START

```
START  filename
```

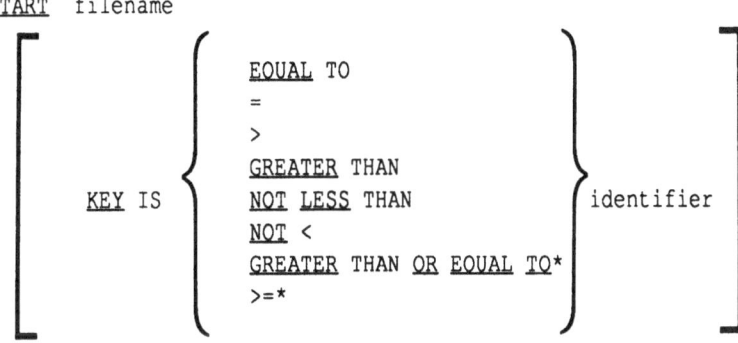

```
         KEY IS  { EQUAL TO                }  identifier
                 { =                       }
                 { >                       }
                 { GREATER THAN            }
                 { NOT LESS THAN           }
                 { NOT <                   }
                 { GREATER THAN OR EQUAL TO*}
                 { >=*                     }

         [INVALID KEY imperative statement ]

         [NOT INVALID KEY imperative-statement ]*
    [END-START]*
```

2.22 STOP

```
STOP  { literal }
      { RUN     }
```

2.23 SUBTRACT

```
(1)  SUBTRACT  { identifier }  ...  FROM {identifier [ROUNDED]} ...
               { literal    }

         [ON SIZE ERROR imperative-statement]

         [NOT ON SIZE ERROR imperative-statement] *

    [END-SUBTRACT] *
```

(2) SUBTRACT { identifier } ... FROM { identifier }
               { literal   }   { literal   }

     GIVING   identifier [ROUNDED]   ...

        [ON SIZE ERROR imperative-statement]

        [NOT ON SIZE ERROR imperative-statement]*

   [END-SUBTRACT]*

2.24 WRITE

(1) WRITE record-name [FROM identifier]

$$\left[\begin{Bmatrix} BEFORE \\ AFTER \end{Bmatrix} \text{ ADVANCING } \left\{ \begin{Bmatrix} identifier \\ integer \\ PAGE \end{Bmatrix} \begin{bmatrix} LINE \\ LINES \end{bmatrix} \right\} \right]$$

$$\left[AT \begin{Bmatrix} END\text{-}OF\text{-}PAGE \\ EOP \end{Bmatrix} \text{ imperative-statement} \right]$$

$$\left[NOT \quad AT \begin{Bmatrix} END\text{-}OF\text{-}PAGE \\ EOP \end{Bmatrix} \text{ imperative-statement*} \right]$$

   [END-WRITE]*

(2) WRITE record-name [FROM identifier]

        [INVALID KEY imperative-statement]

        [NOT INVALID KEY imperative-statement]*

     [END-WRITE]*

Index

WORKING-STORAGE SECTION
  8
WRITE 75, 105, 106, 107, 110, 115
WRITE AFTER 89
WRITE FROM 80, 89